JUMBO
UKULELE
SONGBOOK

ISBN 978-1-4803-4571-3

HAL•LEONARD®
CORPORATION
7777 W. BLUEMOUND RD. P.O.BOX 13819 MILWAUKEE, WI 53213

In Australia Contact:
Hal Leonard Australia Pty. Ltd.
4 Lentara Court
Cheltenham, Victoria, 3192 Australia
Email: ausadmin@halleonard.com.au

Visit Hal Leonard Online at
www.halleonard.com

CONTENTS

After You've Gone

Words by Henry Creamer
Music by Turner Layton

There'll come a time, ____ now don't for - get it.
Af - ter the years ____ we've been to - geth - er,

There'll come a time ____ when you'll re - gret it.
through joy and tears, ____ all kinds of weath - er.

Some - day, when you grow lone - ly,
Some - day, blue and down - heart - ed,

your heart will break like mine and you'll want me on - ly.
you'll long to be with me right back where you start - ed.

Af - ter you've gone, ____ af - ter you've gone a -
Af - ter I'm gone, ____ af - ter I'm gone a -

1.
2.

way. _____
way. _____ ____

Ain't We Got Fun?

Words by Gus Kahn and Raymond B. Egan
Music by Richard A. Whiting

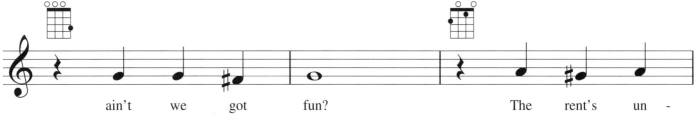

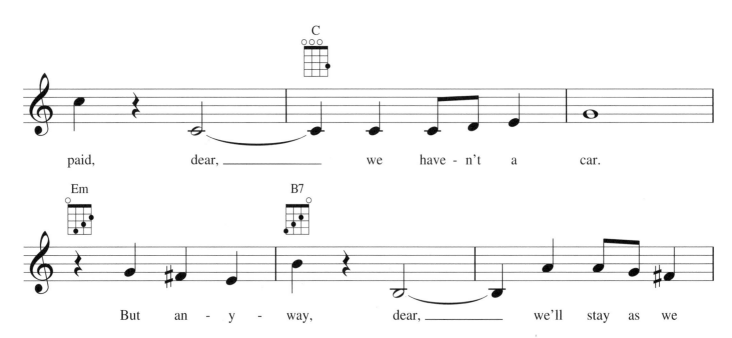

Alabama Jubilee

Words by Jack Yellen
Music by George Cobb

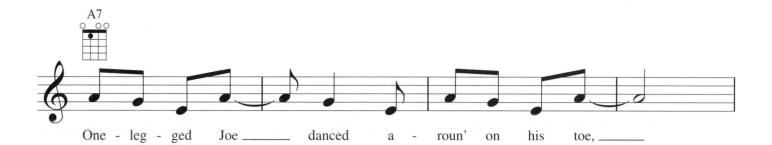

One - leg - ged Joe _____ danced a - roun' on his toe, _____

threw a - way his crutch and hol - lered, "Let 'er go!" _____ Oh, hon - ey,

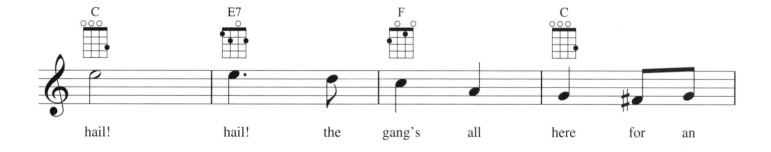

hail! hail! the gang's all here for an

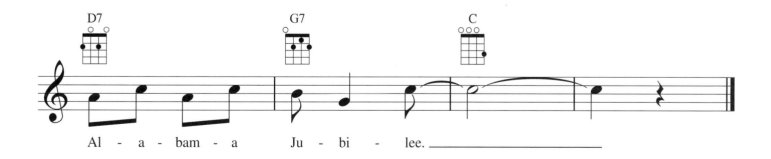

Al - a - bam - a Ju - bi - lee. _____

America, the Beautiful

Words by Katharine Lee Bates
Music by Samuel A. Ward

Additional Lyrics

3. O beautiful for heroes proved
   In liberating strife,
   Who more than self their country loved
   And mercy more than life!
   America! America!
   May God thy gold refine
   'Til all success be nobleness
   And every gain divine.

4. O beautiful for patriot dream
   That sees beyond the years;
   Thine alabaster cities gleam
   Undimmed by human tears.
   America! America!
   God shed His grace on thee,
   And crown thy good with brotherhood
   From sea to shining sea.

Boola! Boola!

By A.M. Hirsch

Avalon

Words by Al Jolson and B.G. DeSylva
Music by Vincent Rose

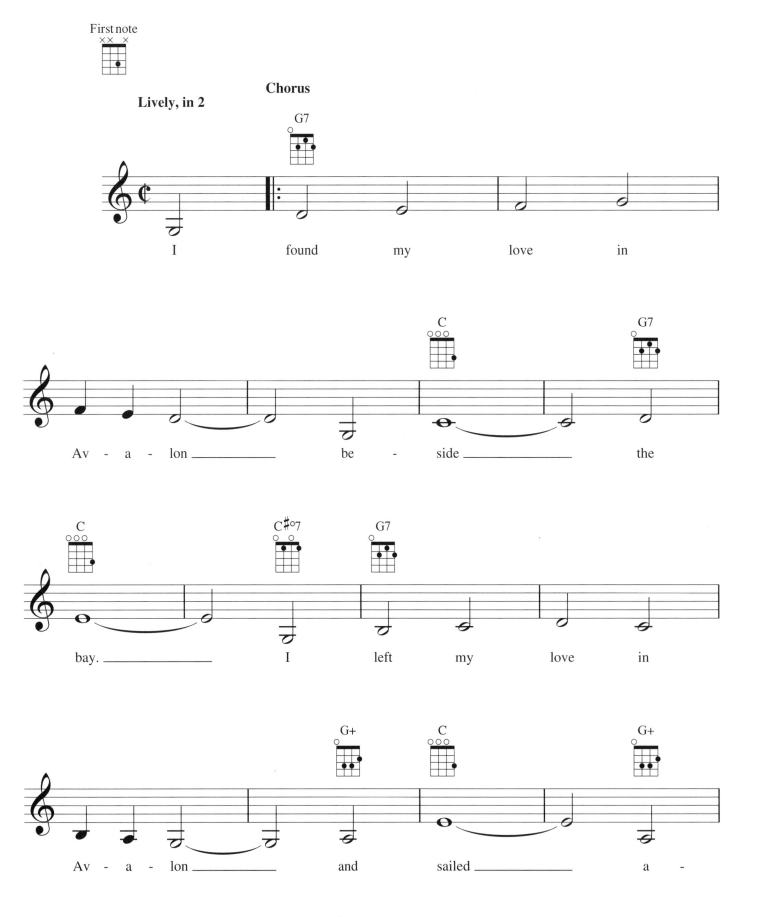

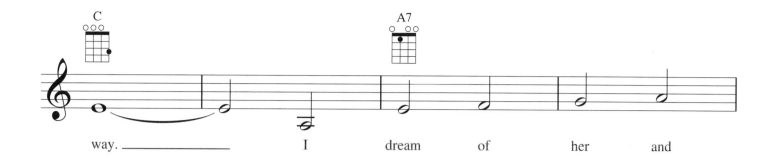

way. _____ I dream of her and

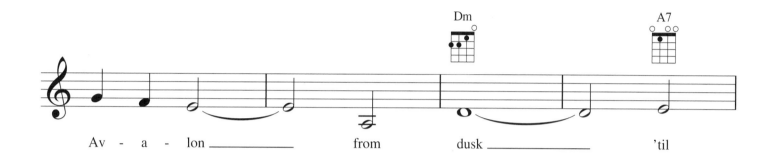

Av - a - lon _____ from dusk _____ 'til

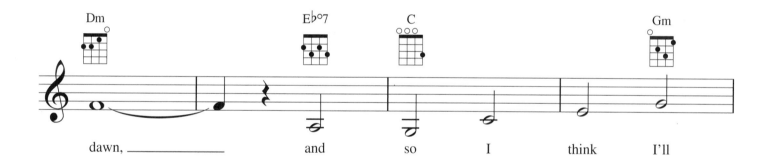

dawn, _____ and so I think I'll

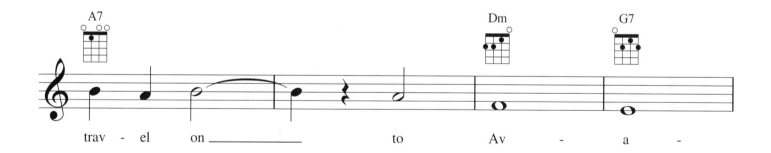

trav - el on _____ to Av - a -

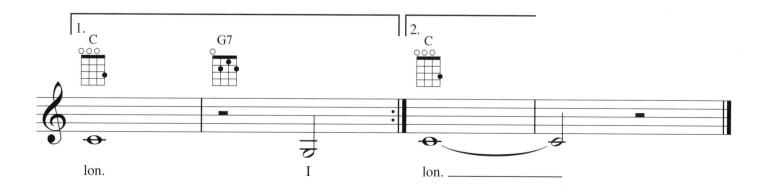

lon. I lon. _____

Baby, Won't You Please Come Home

Words and Music by Charles Warfield and Clarence Williams

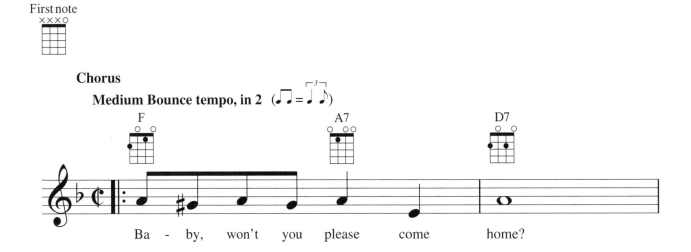

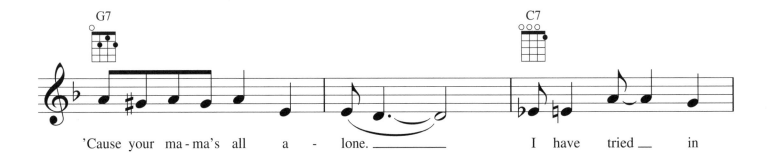

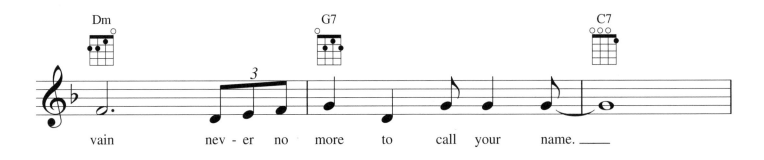

When you left you broke my heart, _____ be - cause I nev - er thought we'd

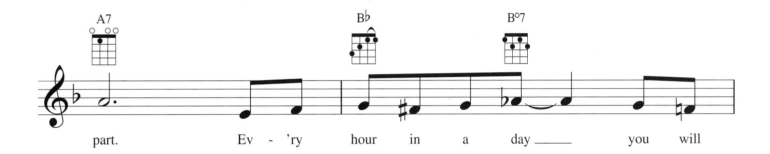

part. Ev - 'ry hour in a day _____ you will

hear me say: __ Ba - by, won't you please come home?

home? Dad - dy needs Ma - ma. Ba - by, won't you please come home? __

Bill Bailey, Won't You Please Come Home

Words and Music by Hughie Cannon

First note

Chorus
Lively, in 2

F
Won't you come home, Bill Bai - ley, won't you come

F°7   C7
home?   I miss you all day long. _____

I'll do the cook - ing, hon - ey, I'll pay the

C+   F
rent.   I know I've done you wrong. _____

'Mem - ber that rain - y eve - ning I drove you

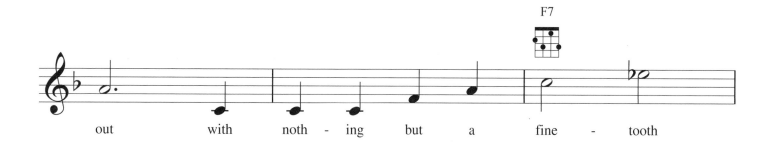

F7

out with noth - ing but a fine - tooth

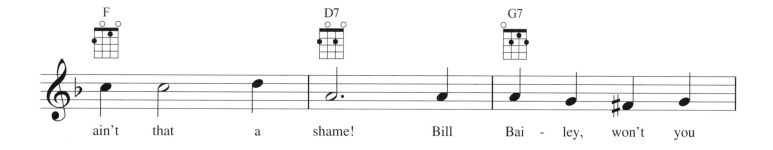

B♭ B°7

comb? _____ I know I'm to blame, well,

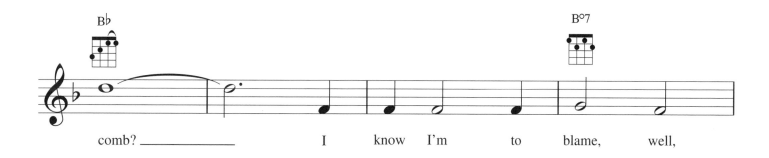

F D7 G7

ain't that a shame! Bill Bai - ley, won't you

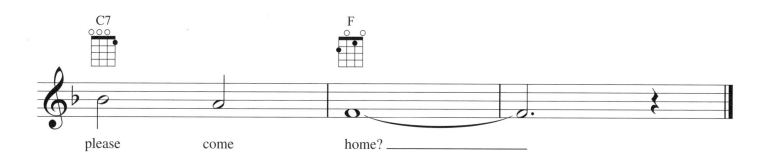

C7 F

please come home? _____

The Bowery

Words by Charles H. Hoyt
Music by Percy Gaunt

Additional Lyrics

3. I went into an auction store;
   I never saw any thieves before.
   First, he sold me a pair of socks,
   Then said he, "How much for the box?"
   Someone said, "Two dollars." I said, "Three!"
   He emptied the box and gave it to me.
   "I sold you the box, not the socks," said he.
   I'll never go there anymore!

4. I went into a concert hall;
   I didn't have a good time at all.
   Just the minute that I sat down,
   Girls began singing, "New Coon in Town."
   I got up mad and spoke out free.
   "Somebody put that man out," said she.
   A man called a bouncer, attended to me.
   I'll never go there anymore!

5. I went into a barber shop;
   He talked till I thought he would never stop.
   I said, "Cut it short," he misunderstood;
   Clipped down my hair just as close as he could.
   He shaved with a razor that scratched like a pin,
   Took off my whiskers and most of my chin.
   That was the worst scrape I ever got in.
   I'll never go there anymore!

6. I struck a place that they called a "dive."
   I was in luck to get out alive.
   When the policeman heard my woes,
   Saw my black eyes and my battered nose,
   "You've been held up!" said the "copper" fly!
   "No sir, but I've been knocked down!" said I.
   Then he laughed, though I couldn't see why!
   I'll never go there anymore!

By the Light of the Silvery Moon

Lyric by Ed Madden
Music by Gus Edwards

Careless Love

Anonymous

The Caissons Go Rolling Along

Words and Music by Edmund L. Gruber

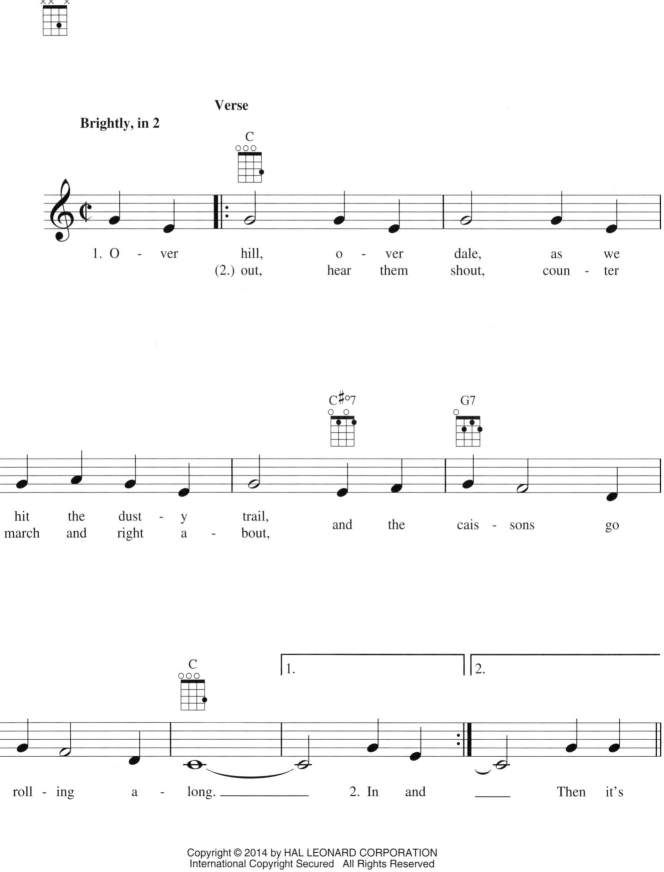

Chorus

hi!   hi!   hee!   in   the   field   ar   -   til   -   ler -

y,   shout   out   your   num - bers   loud   and

strong. _____   For   wher   -   e'er   you   go,

you   will   al   -   ways   know   that   the   cais - sons   go

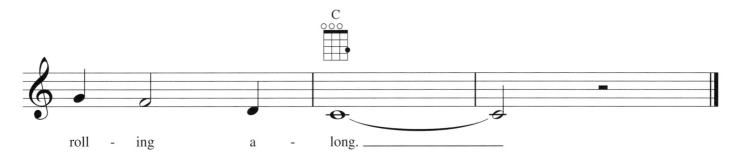

roll - ing   a - long. _____

Carolina in the Morning

Lyrics by Gus Kahn
Music by Walter Donaldson

I long to hear __ once more. 2. Stroll-ing with my girl-ie where the

dew is pearl-y ear-ly in the morn - ing.

But-ter-flies all flut-ter up and kiss each lit-tle but-ter-cup at dawn -

Outro

ing. If I had A-lad-din's lamp for on-ly a day, __

I'd make a wish and here's what I'd say: __ Noth-ing could be fin-er than to

be in Car-o-li-na in the morn - ing.

C.C. Rider

Traditional

First note

Verse
Blues

1. C.   C.   rid - er, _____   see what you have done? ___
2. Tell me,   rid - er: _____   what is on your mind? ___

_____   C.   C.   rid - er,   see what you have done? ___
_____   Tell me,   rid - er: what is on your mind? ___

_____   You   made   me   love   you,
_____   Oh,   tell   me   why   you

now   your   friend   has   come. ____
treat   me   so   un - kind. ____

Chinatown, My Chinatown

Words by William Jerome
Music by Jean Schwartz

(Oh, My Darling)
Clementine

Words and Music by Percy Montrose

First note

Verse

Moderately

1. In a cav - ern, in a can - yon, ex - ca - vat - ing for a
2. Light she was, and like a fair - y, and her shoes were num - ber
3. Drove she duck - lings to the wa - ter ev - 'ry morn - ing just at
4. Ru - by lips a - bove the wa - ter, blow - ing bub - bles soft and

mine, dwelt a min - er, for - ty - nin - er, and his
nine, her - ring box - es with - out top - ses, san - dals
nine, hit her foot a - gainst a splin - ter, fell in -
fine, a - las for me I was no swim - mer, so I

Chorus

daugh - ter, Clem - en - tine.
were for Clem - en - tine.
to the foam - ing brine.
lost my Clem - en - tine.

Oh, my dar - ling, oh, my

dar - ling, oh, my dar - ling, Clem - en - tine, you are

lost and gone for - ev - er. Dread - ful sor - ry, Clem - en - tine.

Far Above Cayuga's Waters

Lyrics by A.C. Weekes and W.M. Smith
Music by H.S. Thompson

Cockles and Mussels
(Molly Malone)

Traditional Irish Folksong

First note

Warmly   Verse

1. In   Dub - lin's   fair   cit - y,   where   girls   are   so
(2.) was   a   fish - mon - ger,   but   sure   'twas   no
(3.) died   of   a   fe - ver,   and   no   one   could

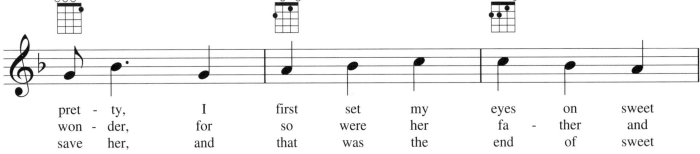

pret - ty,   I   first   set   my   eyes   on   sweet
won - der,   for   so   were   her   fa - ther   and
save   her,   and   that   was   the   end   of   sweet

Mol - ly   Ma - lone.   As   she   pushed   her   wheel -
moth - er   be - fore.   And   they   pushed   each   wheeled   their
Mol - ly   Ma - lone.   But   her   ghost   wheels   her

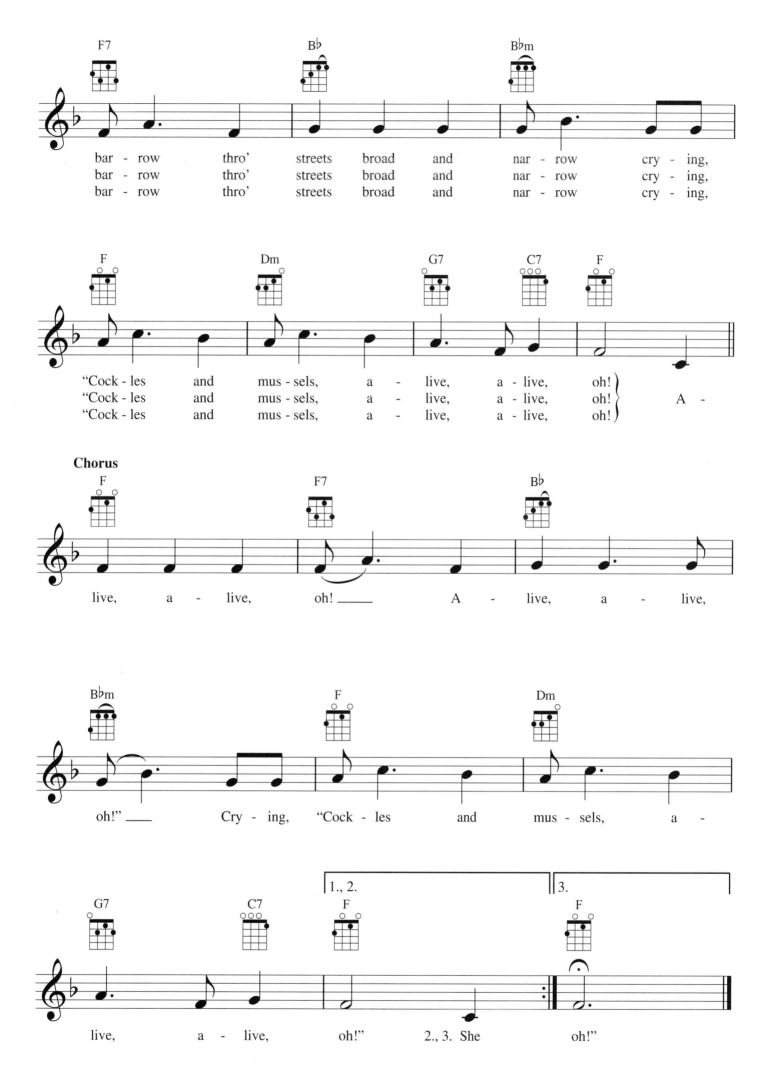

F7   B♭   B♭m

bar - row   thro'   streets   broad   and   nar - row   cry - ing,
bar - row   thro'   streets   broad   and   nar - row   cry - ing,
bar - row   thro'   streets   broad   and   nar - row   cry - ing,

F   Dm   G7   C7   F

"Cock - les   and   mus - sels,   a - live,   a - live,   oh!
"Cock - les   and   mus - sels,   a - live,   a - live,   oh!   A -
"Cock - les   and   mus - sels,   a - live,   a - live,   oh!

Chorus

F   F7   B♭

live,   a - live,   oh! _____   A - live,   a - live,

B♭m   F   Dm

oh!" ___   Cry - ing,   "Cock - les   and   mus - sels,   a -

|1., 2. |3.

G7   C7   F   F

live,   a - live,   oh!"   2., 3. She   oh!"

Danny Boy

Words by Frederick Edward Weatherly
Traditional Irish Folk Melody

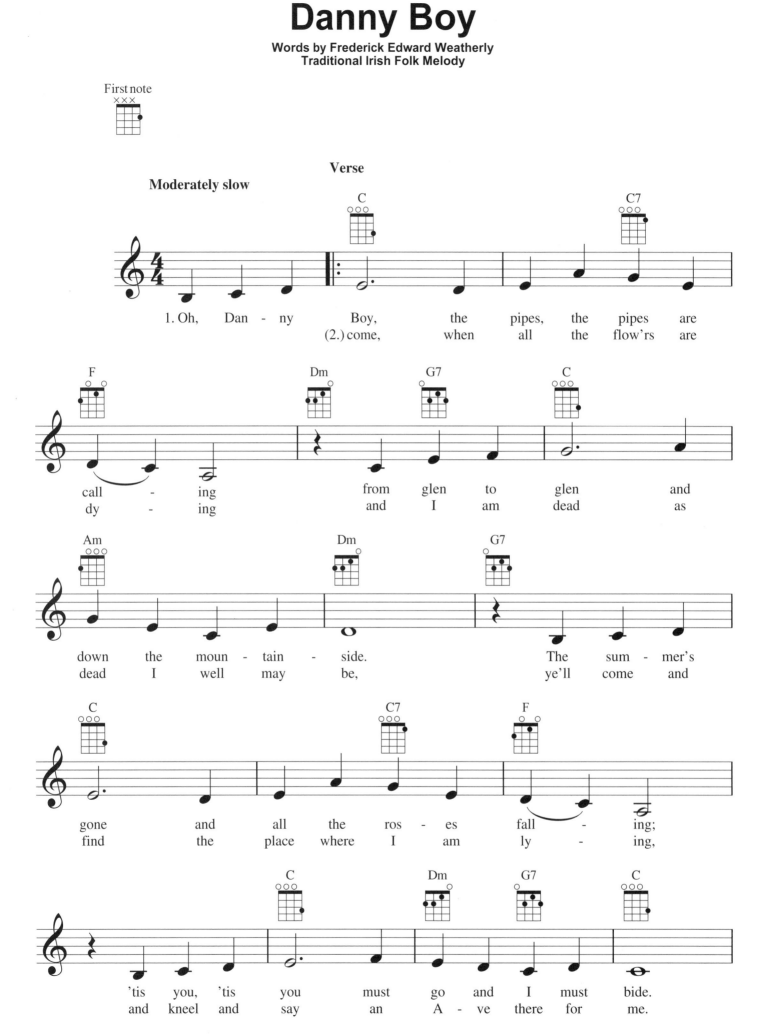

Do Lord

Traditional

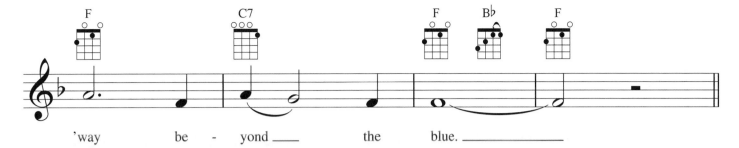

'way   be - yond _____   the   blue. _____

Chorus

Do   Lord,   oh,   do   Lord,   oh,   do   re - mem - ber

me.   Do   Lord,   oh,   do   Lord,   oh,   do   re - mem - ber

me.   Do   Lord,   oh,   do   Lord,   oh,   do   re - mem - ber

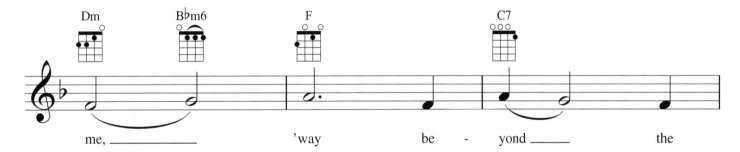

me, _____   'way   be - yond _____   the

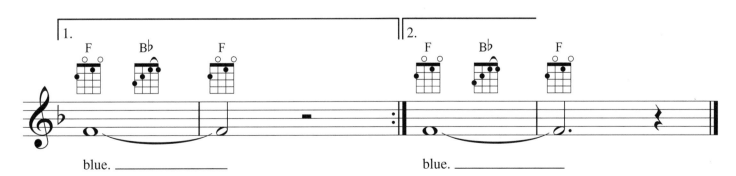

blue. _____   blue. _____

Down by the Old Mill Stream

Words and Music by Tell Taylor

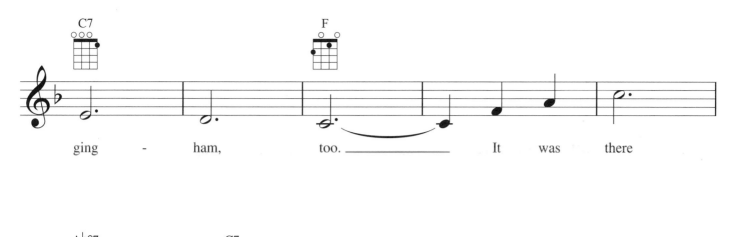

ging - ham, too. _____ It was there

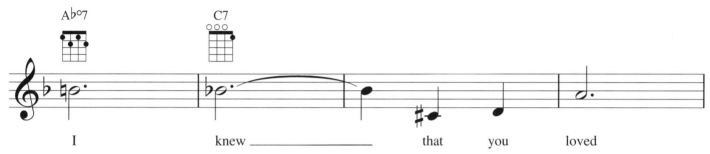

I knew _____ that you loved

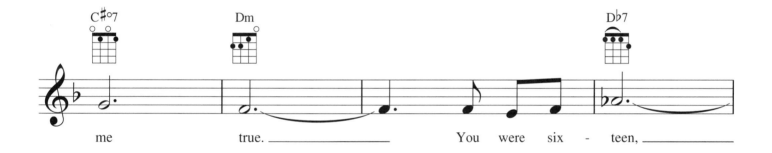

me true. _____ You were six - teen, _____

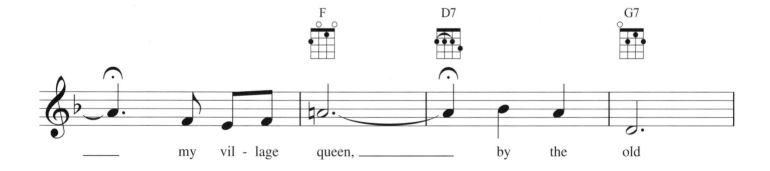

_____ my vil - lage queen, _____ by the old

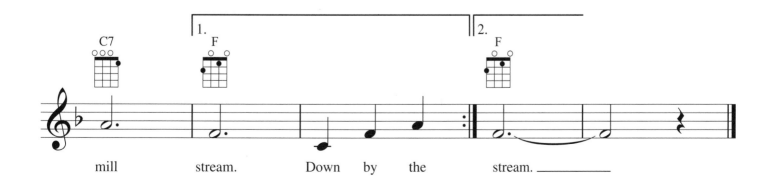

1.

2.

mill stream. Down by the stream. _____

Down by the Riverside

African-American Spiritual

1. Gon-na   lay   down   my   bur - den ___
(2.) lay   down   my   sword   and   shield down   by   the
(3.) try   on   my   long   white   robe

riv - er - side, ___   down   by   the   riv - er - side, ___

down   by   the   riv - er - side. ___   Gon - na   lay   down   my
Gon - na   lay   down   my
Gon - na   try   on   my

bur - den ___   down   by   the   riv - er - side ___   and
sword   and   shield
long   white   robe

stud - y _____   war   no   more.

Chorus

Down Yonder

Words and Music by L. Wolfe Gilbert

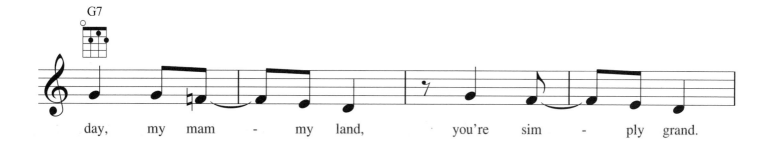

day, my mam - my land, you're sim - ply grand.

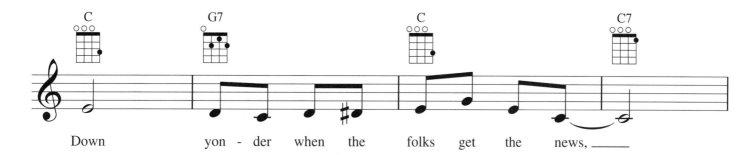

Down yon - der when the folks get the news, _____

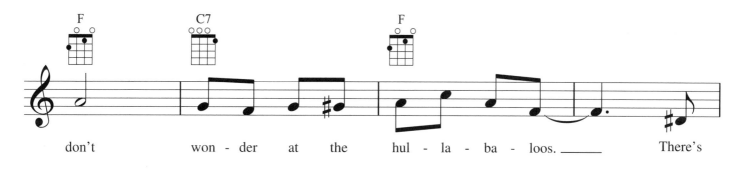

don't won - der at the hul - la - ba - loos. _____ There's

dad - dy and mam - my, there's Eph - raim and Sam -

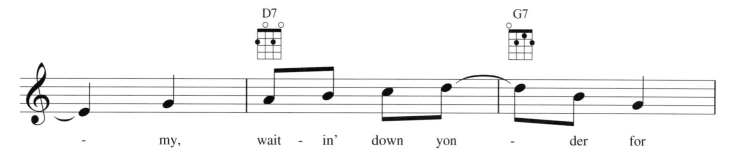

- my, wait - in' down yon - der for

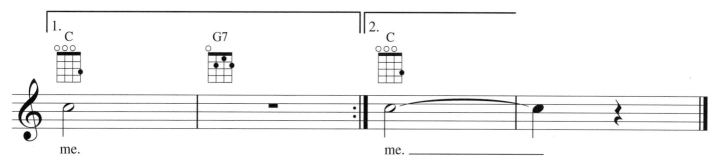

1. me.

2. me. _____

Fascination
(Valse Tzigane)
By F.D. Marchetti

First note
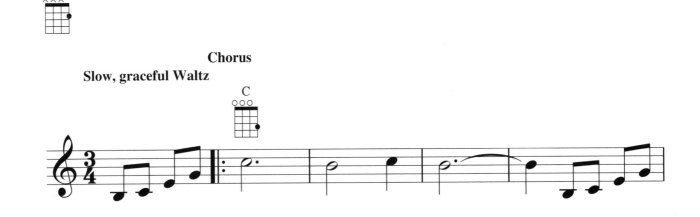

Chorus

Slow, graceful Waltz

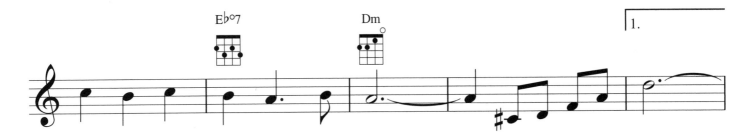

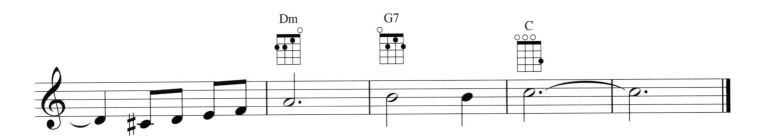

Frankie and Johnny

Anonymous Blues Ballad

First note

Verse

Moderately

1. Frank - ie and John - ny were lov - ers,
2. Frank - ie and John - ny went walk - ing,
3. John - ny said, "I've ____ got to leave now,
4.–6. *See additional lyrics*

said they were real - ly in love. Now, Frank - ie was true ____ to her
John - ny had on ____ a new suit that Frank - ie had bought _ with a
but I won't be ____ ver - y long. Don't sit up and wait ____ for me,

John - ny, true as all the stars a - bove.
"c - note," 'cause it made him look so cute. } He was her man, ____
hon - ey; don't you wor - ry while I'm gone." }

1.–5.

6.

____ but he done her wrong. ____

Additional Lyrics

4. Frankie went down to the hotel,
   Looked in the window so high.
   There she saw her lovin' Johnny
   Making love to Nellie Bly.
   He was her man,
   But he done her wrong.

5. Johnny saw Frankie a-comin';
   Down the back stairs he did scoot.
   Frankie, she took out her pistol;
   Oh, that lady sure could shoot!
   He was her man,
   But he done her wrong.

6. Frankie, she went to the big chair,
   Calm as a lady could be.
   Turning her eyes up, she whispered,
   "Lord, I'm coming up to Thee.
   He was my man,
   But he done me wrong."

For He's a Jolly Good Fellow

Traditional

First note

Chorus
Lively

| C | | | F | C | G7 |

For he's a jol - ly good fel - low, for he's a

| C | | | | | C7 |

jol - ly good fel - low, for ___ he's a jol - ly good

| F | | | C | G7 | C |

fel - low, which no - bod - y can de - ny. ___

Bridge

| C | | F | | C |

___ Which no - bod - y can de - ny, ___ which

Copyright © 2011 by HAL LEONARD CORPORATION
International Copyright Secured   All Rights Reserved

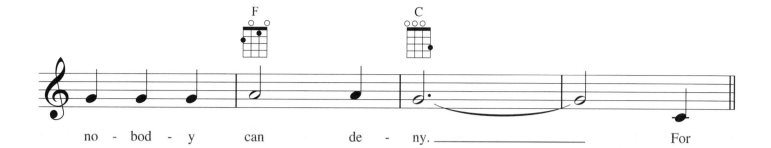

no - bod - y can de - ny. _____ For

Chorus

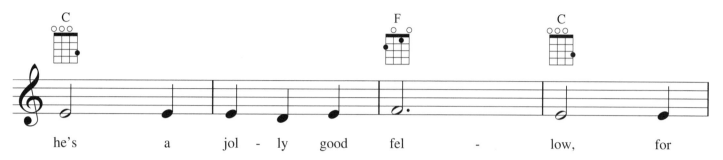

he's a jol - ly good fel - low, for

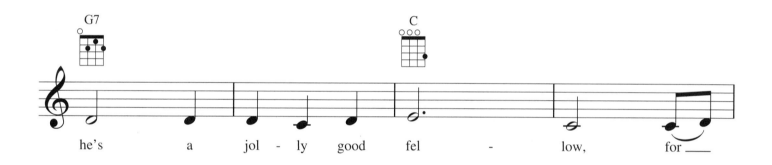

he's a jol - ly good fel - low, for ___

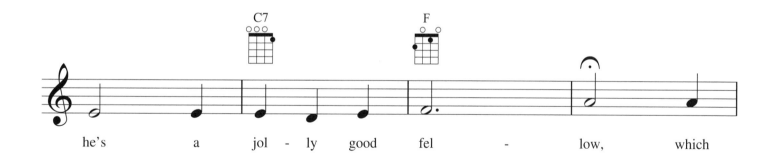

he's a jol - ly good fel - low, which

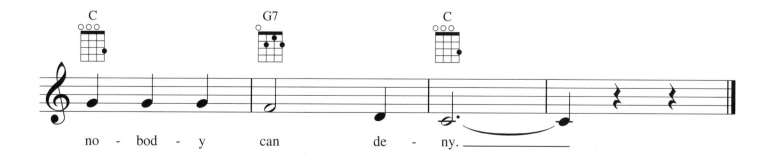

no - bod - y can de - ny. _____

For Me and My Gal

Words by Edgar Leslie and E. Ray Goetz
Music by George W. Meyer

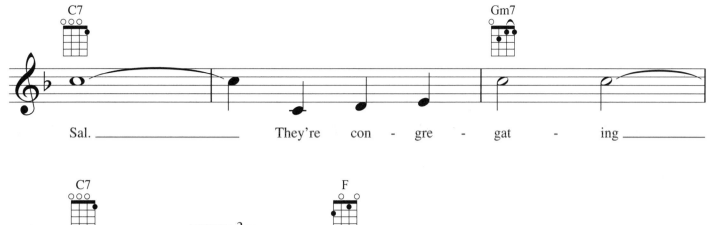

Sal. _____ They're con - gre - gat - ing _____

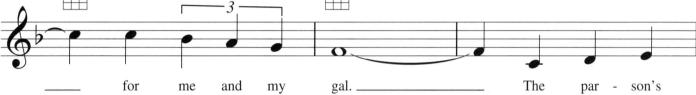

_____ for me and my gal. _____ The par - son's

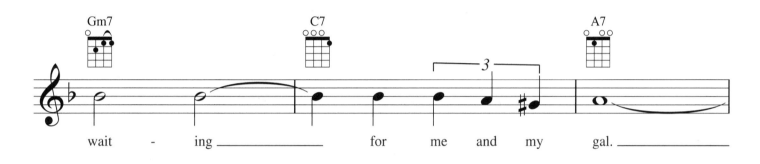

wait - ing _____ for me and my gal. _____

_____ And some - time I'm goin' to build a lit - tle home for two, ___ for

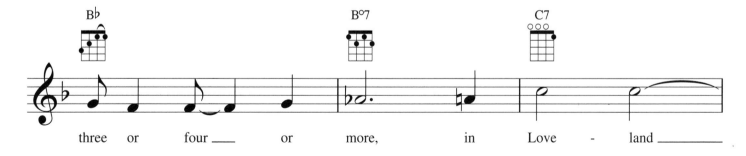

three or four ___ or more, in Love - land _____

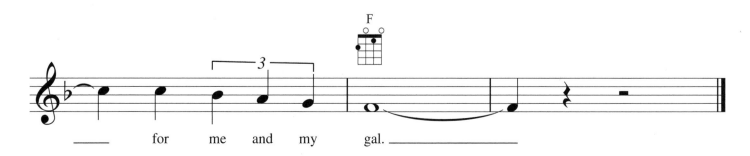

_____ for me and my gal. _____

Freight Train

Words and Music by Elizabeth Cotten

Give Me That Old Time Religion

Traditional

Give My Regards to Broadway

Words and Music by George M. Cohan

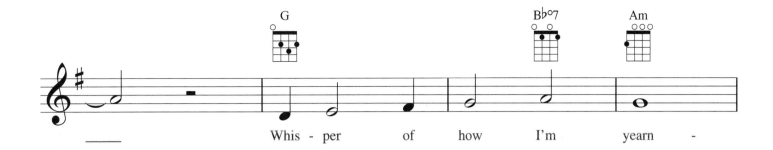

Whis - per   of   how   I'm   yearn -

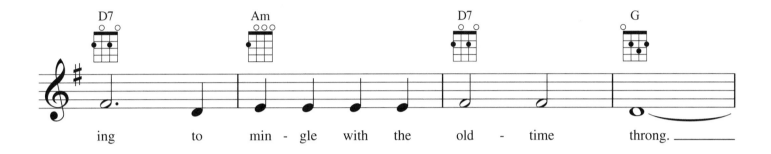

ing   to   min - gle   with   the   old - time   throng. _____

_____   Give   my   re - gards   to   old   Broad -

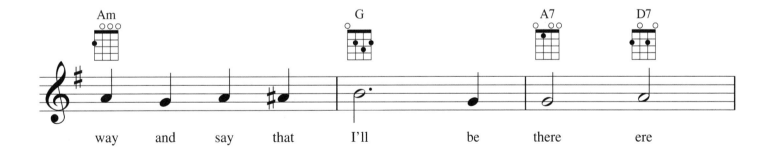

way   and   say   that   I'll   be   there   ere

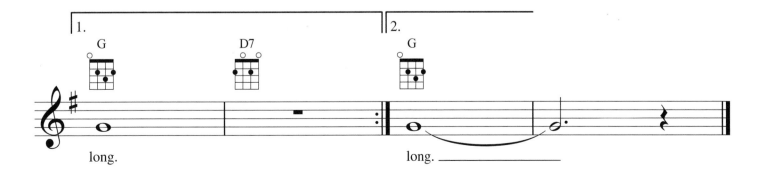

long.   long. _____

Good Night Ladies

Words by E.P. Christy
Traditional Music

Hail, Hail, the Gang's All Here

Words by D.A. Esrom
Music by Theodore F. Morse and Arthur Sullivan

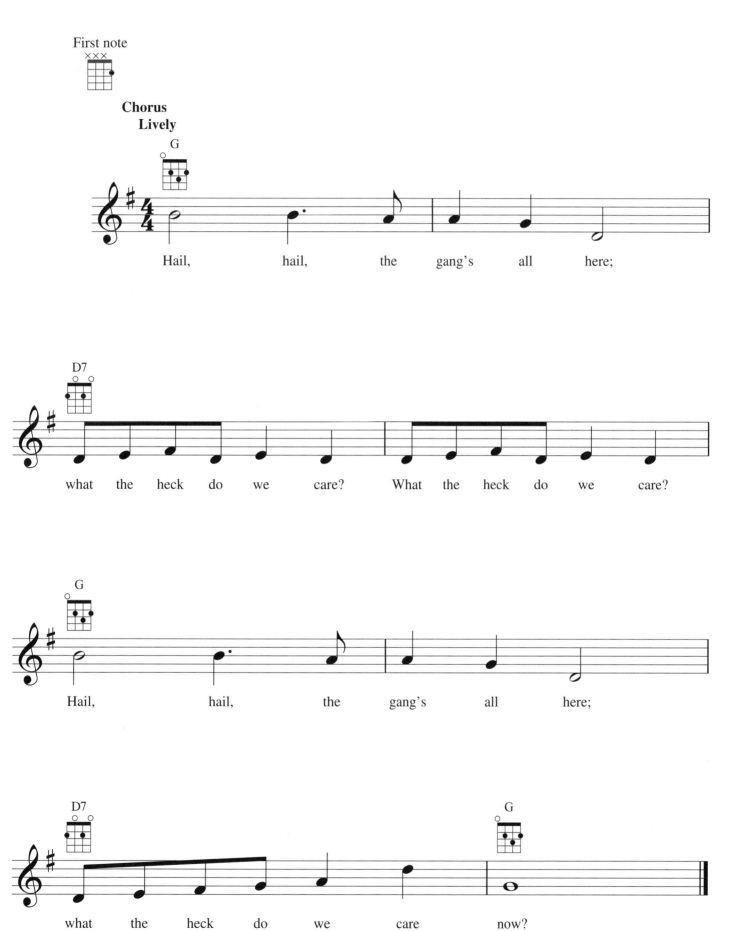

He's Got the Whole World in His Hands

Traditional Spiritual

in His hands. ___ He's got the wind and the rain ___

in His hands. ___ He's got the whole world in His

Verse

hands.   3. He's got   ev-'ry-bod-y here ___   in His   hands. _ He's got

ev-'ry-bod-y here ___   in His   hands. _ He's got   ev-'ry-bod-y here ___

in His   hands. _ He's got the   whole   world   in His   hands.

Hello! Ma Baby

Words by Ida Emerson
Music by Joseph E. Howard

(There'll Be)
A Hot Time in the Old Town Tonight

Words by Joe Hayden
Music by Theodore M. Metz

Hindustan

Words and Music by Oliver Wallace and Harold Weeks

Hin - du - stan, _____ where we

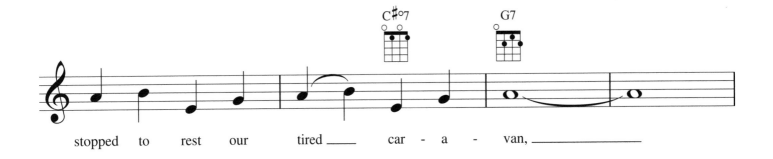

stopped to rest our tired _____ car - a - van, _____

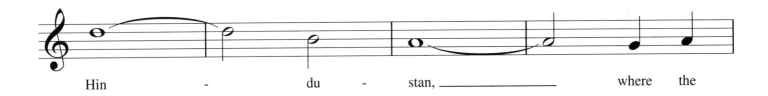

Hin - du - stan, _____ where the

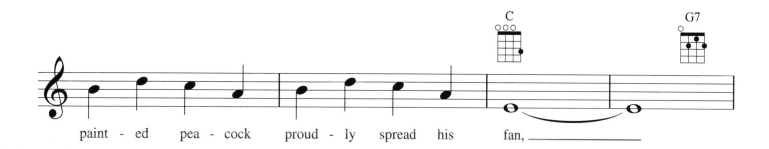

painted pea - cock proud - ly spread his fan, _____

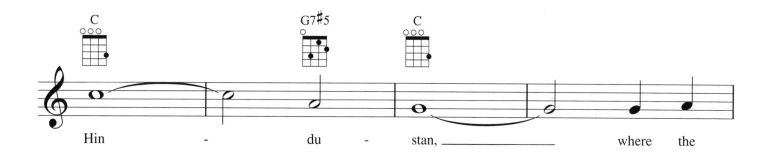

Hin - du - stan, _____ where the

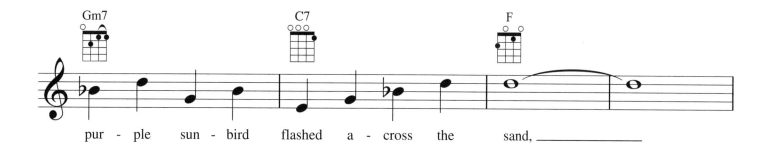

pur - ple sun - bird flashed a - cross the sand, _____

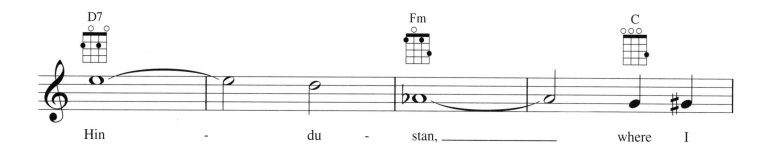

Hin - du - stan, _____ where I

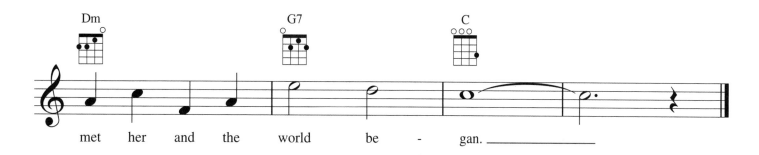

met her and the world be - gan. _____

House of the Rising Sun

Southern American Folksong

Additional Lyrics

3. My mother, she's a tailor,
   She sells those new blue jeans.
   My sweetheart, he's a drunkard, Lord,
   Drink down in New Orleans.

4. The only thing a drunkard needs
   Is a suitcase and a trunk.
   The only time he's satisfied
   Is when he's on a drunk.

5. Go tell my baby sister,
   Never do like I have done,
   To shun that house in New Orleans
   They call the Rising Sun.

6. One foot is on the platform,
   And the other is on the train.
   I'm going back to New Orleans
   To wear the ball and chain.

7. I'm going back to New Orleans,
   My race is almost run.
   Going back to end my life
   Beneath the Rising Sun.

I Love You Truly

Words and Music by Carrie Jacobs-Bond

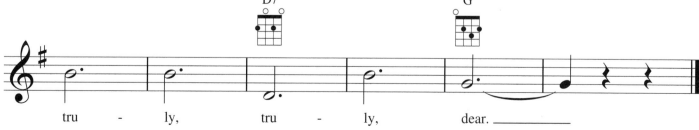

I Ain't Got Nobody
(And Nobody Cares for Me)

Words by Roger Graham
Music by Spencer Williams and Dave Peyton

First note

Chorus
Moderately, in 2

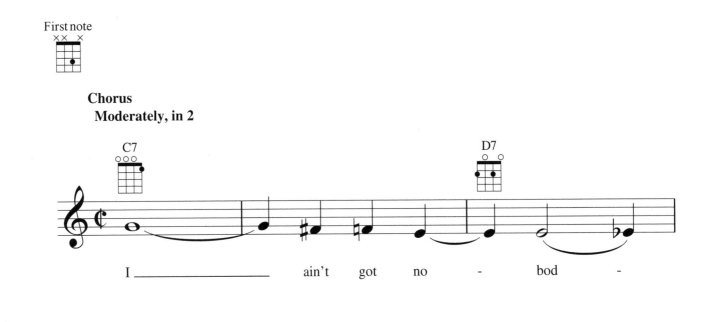

I _____ ain't got no - bod -

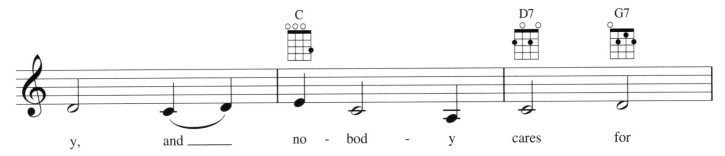

y, and _____ no - bod - y cares for

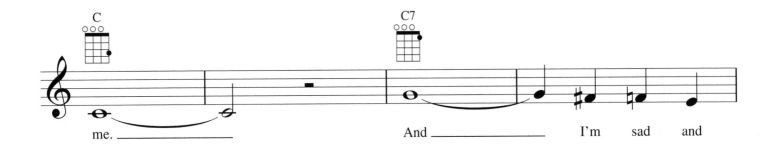

me. _____ And _____ I'm sad and

lone - ly; won't some - bod - y

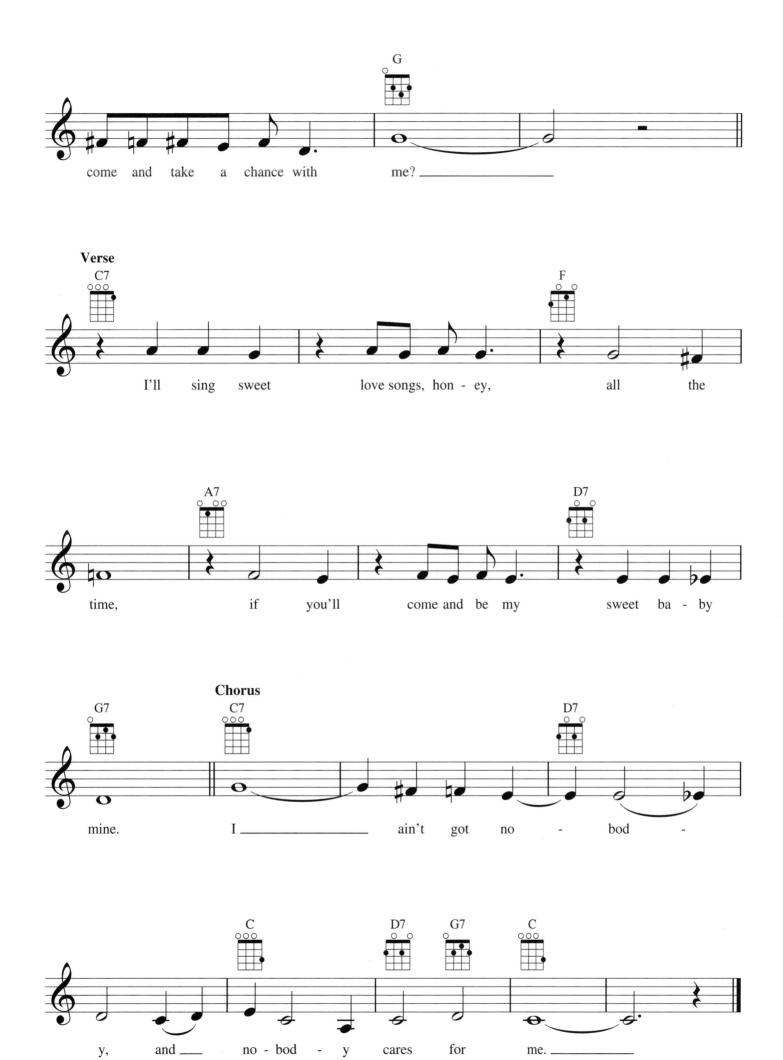

come and take a chance with me? _____

Verse

I'll sing sweet love songs, hon - ey, all the

time, if you'll come and be my sweet ba - by

Chorus

mine. I _____ ain't got no - bod -

y, and ___ no - bod - y cares for me. _____

I Want a Girl
(Just Like the Girl That Married Dear Old Dad)

Words by William Dillon
Music by Harry von Tilzer

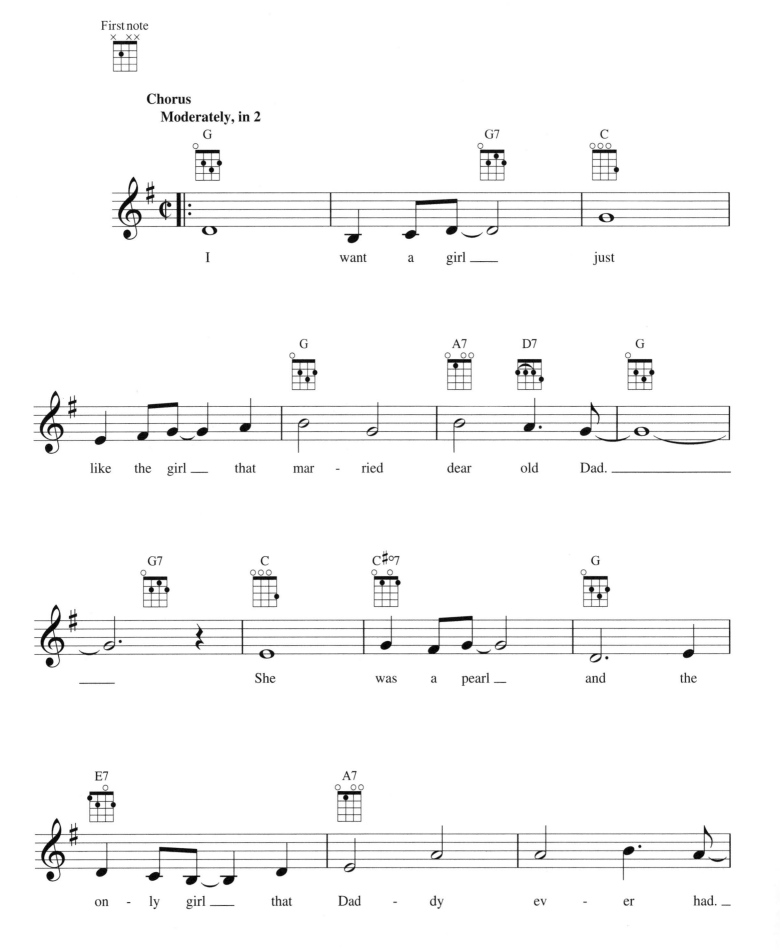

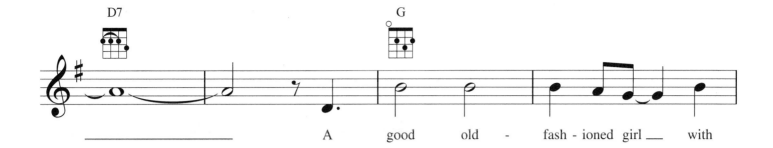

A good old - fash - ioned girl ___ with

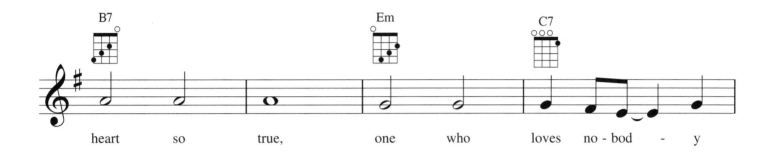

heart so true, one who loves no - bod - y

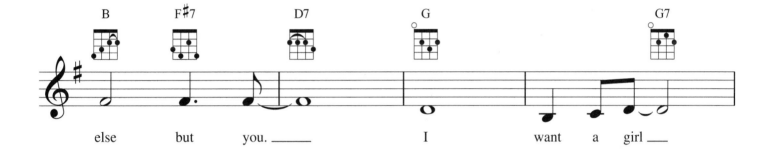

else but you. ___ I want a girl ___

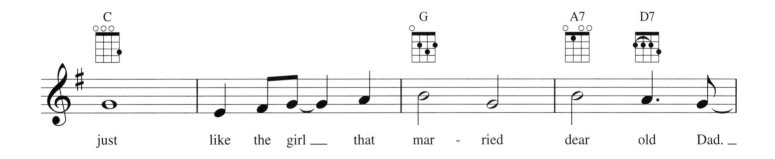

just like the girl ___ that mar - ried dear old Dad. __

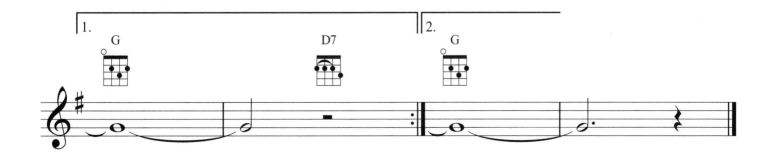

I Wish I Was Single Again

Words and Music by J.C. Beckel

First note

Verse
Moderately

1. I wish I was sin - gle, oh then, oh then, __ I
2. I mar - ried a wife, __ oh then, oh then, __ I
3. My wife __ took sick, __ oh then, oh then, __ my
4.–7. *See additional lyrics*

wish I was sin - gle, oh then. _____ When I was sin - gle, my
mar - ried a wife, __ oh then. _____ I mar - ried a wife, she's the
wife __ took sick, __ oh then. _____ My wife took sick, I went for the

pock - ets did jin - gle, and I wish I was sin - gle a - gain. _____
plague of my life, __ I __ wish I was sin - gle a - gain. _____
doc - tor right quick, __ I __ wish I was sin - gle a - gain. _____

Additional Lyrics

4. My wife, she died, oh then, oh then,
   My wife, she died, oh then.
   My wife, she died, dang little cared I,
   To think I was single again.

5. I married another, oh then, oh then,
   I married another, oh then.
   I married another, she's the devil's stepmother,
   And I wish I was single again.

6. She beat me, she banged me, oh then, oh then,
   She beat me, she banged me, oh then.
   She beat me, she banged me, she swore she would hang me,
   I wish I was single again.

7. She got the rope, oh then, oh then,
   She got the rope, oh then.
   She got the rope and she greased it with soap,
   And I wish I was single again.

In the Good Old Summertime

Words by Ren Shields
Music by George Evans

First note

With a lilt

Verse

1. There's a   time in each year that we
(2.) swim in the pool you'd play

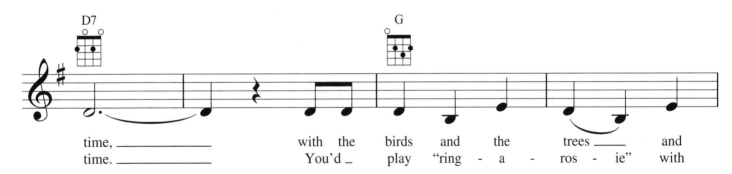

al - ways hold dear, good old sum - mer -
"hook - y" from school, good old sum - mer -

time, _____ with the birds and the trees ____ and
time. _____ You'd _ play "ring - a - ros - ie" with

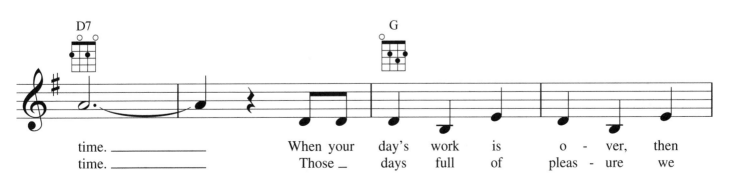

sweet - scent - ed breez - es, good old sum - mer -
Jim, Kate and Jo - sie, good old sum - mer -

time. _____ When your day's work is o - ver, then
time. _____ Those _ days full of pleas - ure we

you are in clo - ver and life is one beau - ti - ful
now fond - ly treas - ure, when we nev - er thought it a

rhyme. _____ No trou - ble an - noy - ing, each
crime _____ to go steal - ing cher - ries with

one is en - joy - ing the good old sum - mer -
face brown as ber - ries, _____ good old sum - mer -

Chorus

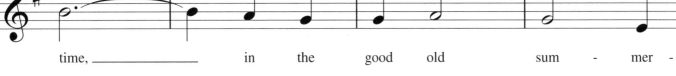

time. _____ In the good old sum - mer -
time. _____

time, _____ in the good old sum - mer -

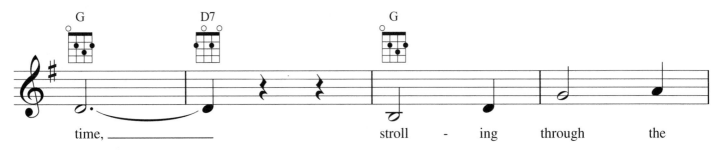

time, _____ stroll - ing through the

68

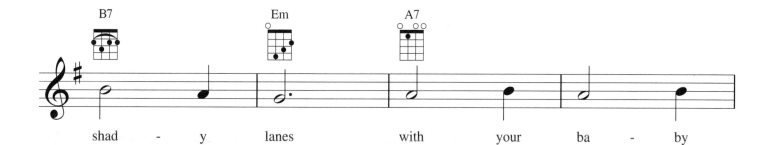

shad - y lanes with your ba - by

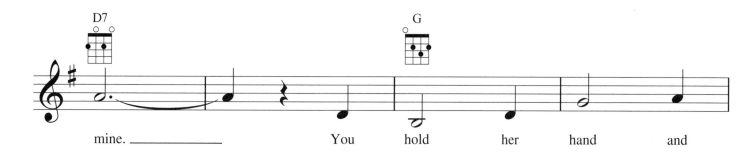

mine. _____ You hold her hand and

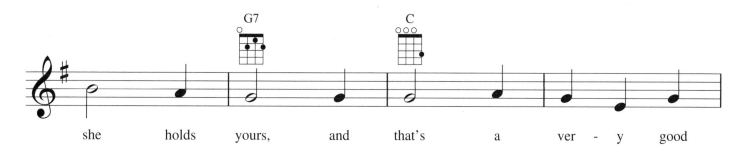

she holds yours, and that's a ver - y good

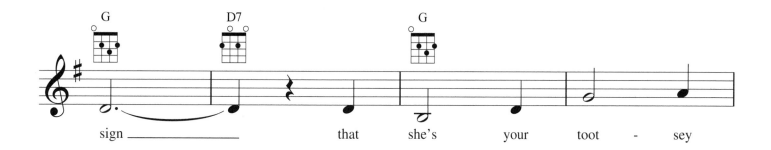

sign _____ that she's your toot - sey

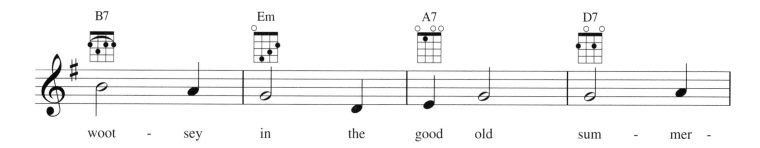

woot - sey in the good old sum - mer -

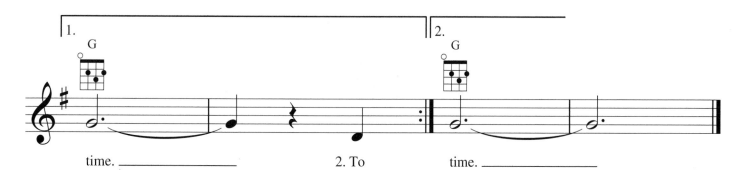

time. _____ 2. To time. _____

I Wonder Who's Kissing Her Now

Lyrics by Will M. Hough and Frank R. Adams
Music by Joseph E. Howard and Harold Orlob

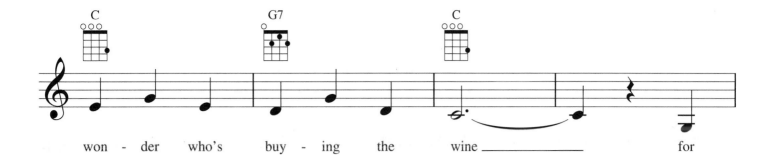

won - der who's buy - ing the wine _____ for

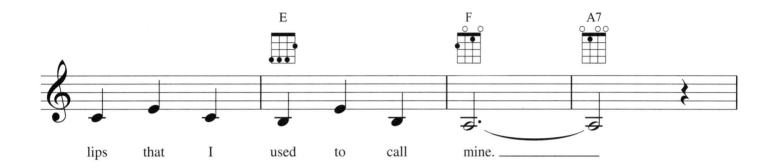

lips that I used to call mine. _____

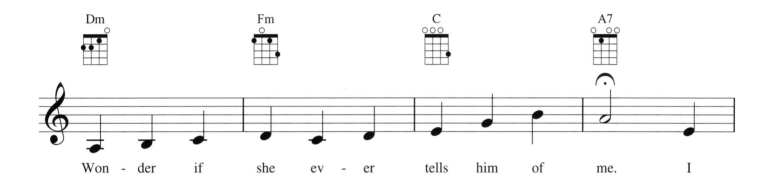

Won - der if she ev - er tells him of me. I

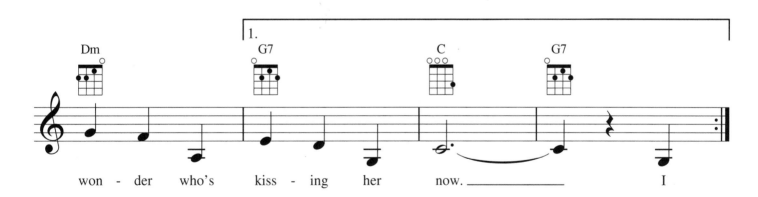

1.

won - der who's kiss - ing her now. _____ I

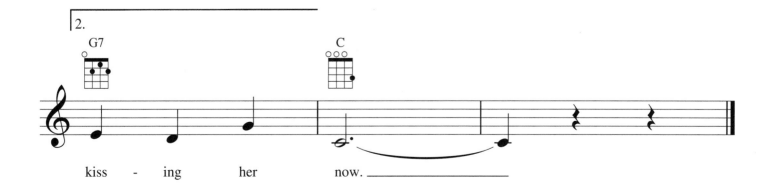

2.

kiss - ing her now. _____

I'll Be with You in Apple Blossom Time

Words by Neville Fleeson
Music by Albert von Tilzer

First note

Chorus
Tenderly

I'll be with you in ap - ple blos - som

time. I'll be with you to change your name to

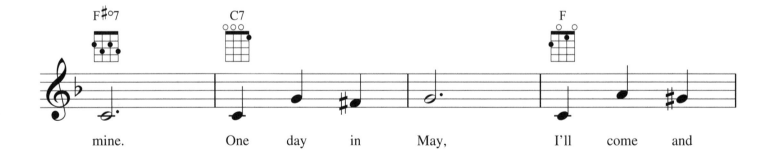

mine. One day in May, I'll come and

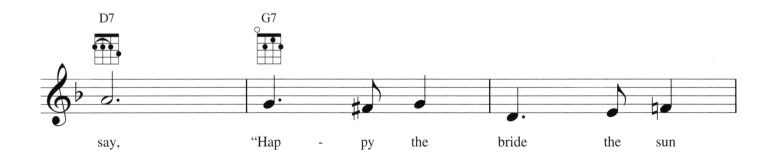

say, "Hap - py the bride the sun

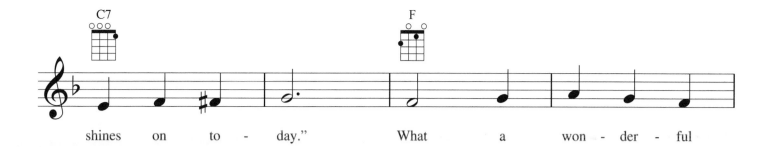

shines   on   to - day."   What   a   won - der - ful

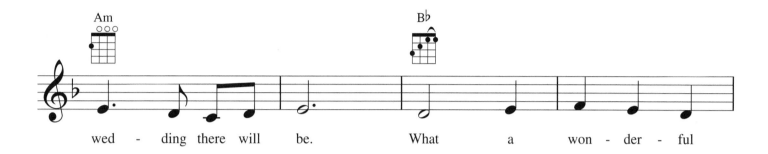

wed - ding there will   be.   What   a   won - der - ful

day   for   you and   me.   Church - bells   will   chime,

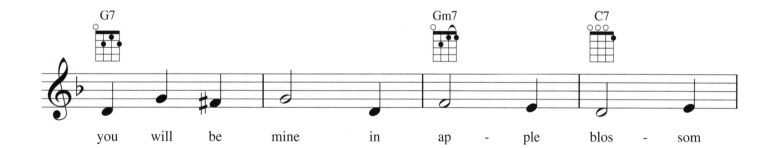

you   will   be   mine   in   ap - ple   blos - som

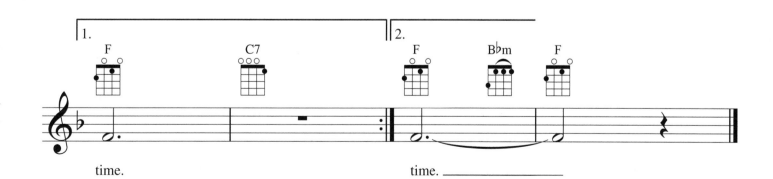

1.   time.   2.   time. _____

I'm Always Chasing Rainbows

Words by Joseph McCarthy
Music by Harry Carroll

First note

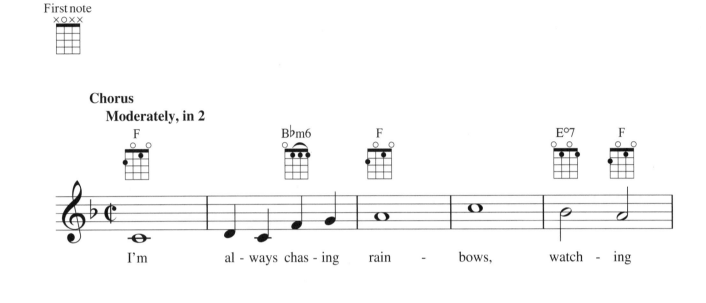

I'm al - ways chas - ing rain - bows, watch - ing

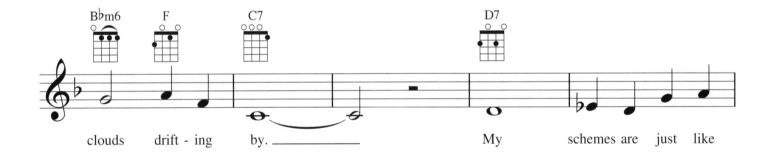

clouds drift - ing by. _____ My schemes are just like

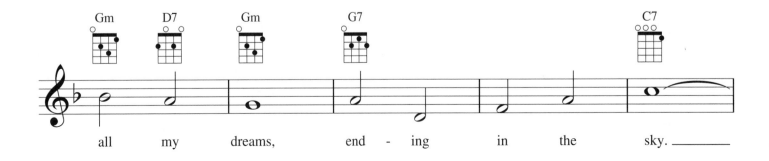

all my dreams, end - ing in the sky. _____

Some fel-lows look and find the sun-shine; I

al - ways look and find the rain. Some fel-lows make a win-ning

some - time; I nev - er e - ven make a gain, be - lieve me.

I'm al - ways chas - ing rain - bows,

wait - ing to find a lit - tle blue - bird in vain. _____

In the Shade of the Old Apple Tree

Words by Harry H. Williams
Music by Egbert Van Alstyne

Let Me Call You Sweetheart

Words by Beth Slater Whitson
Music by Leo Friedman

Indiana
(Back Home Again in Indiana)

Words by Ballard MacDonald
Music by James F. Hanley

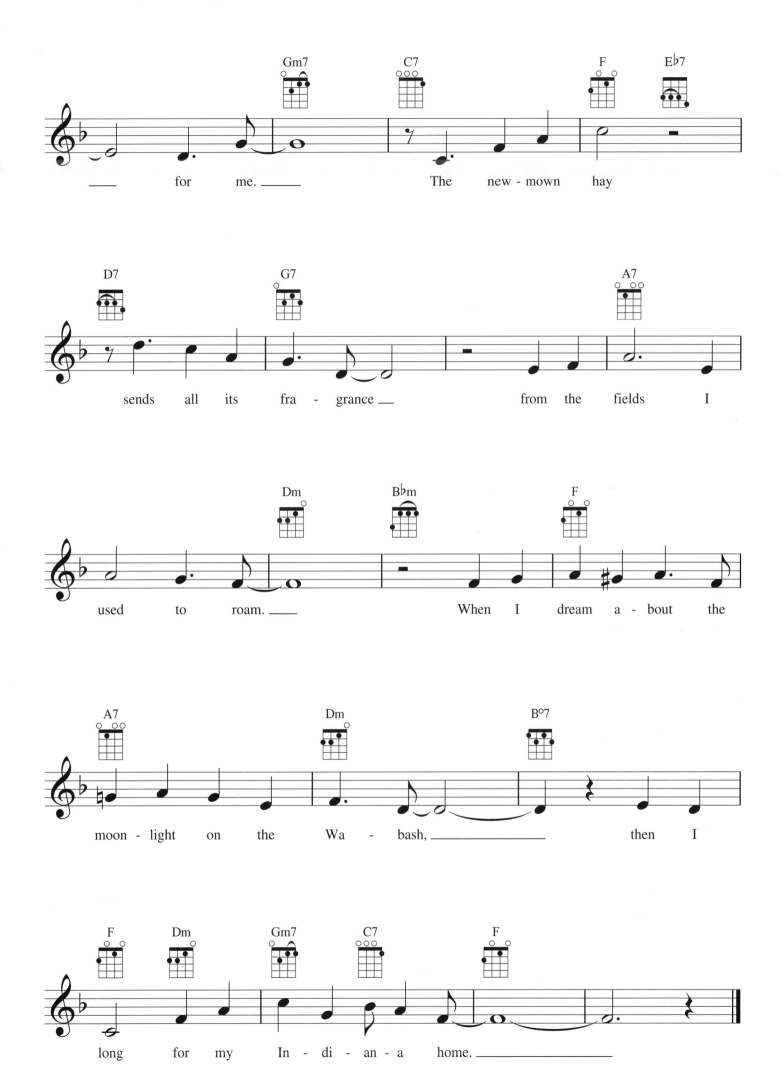

Just a Closer Walk with Thee

Traditional
Arranged by Kenneth Morris

First note

Verse
Moderately

1. I am weak, but Thou art strong.
2. Through this world of toil and snares,
3. When my fee - ble life is o'er,

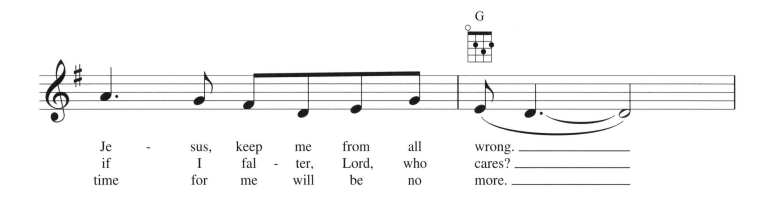

Je - sus, keep me from all wrong. _____
if I fal - ter, Lord, who cares? _____
time for me will be no more. _____

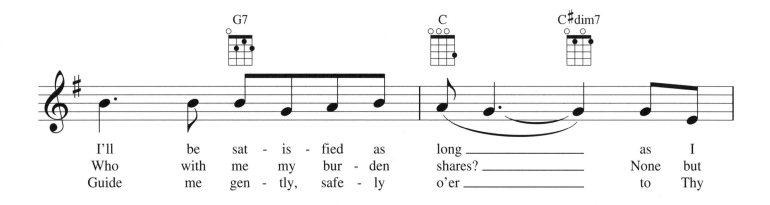

I'll be sat - is - fied as long _____ as I
Who with me my bur - den shares? _____ None but
Guide me gen - tly, safe - ly o'er _____ to Thy

walk, let me walk close to Thee.
Thee, dear &underline{ } Lord, none but Thee.
king - dom &underline{ } shore, to Thy shore.

Chorus

Just a clos - er walk with Thee;

grant it, Je - sus, is my plea. &underline{   }

Dai - ly walk - ing close to Thee, &underline{   } let it

be, dear Lord, let it be.

Listen to the Mockingbird

Words by Alice Hawthorne
Music by Richard Milburn

val - ley, she's sleep - ing in the ___ val - ley, and the

tem - ber, 'twas in the mild Sep - tem - ber, and the

mock - ing - bird is sing - ing where she lies.

mock - ing - bird was sing - ing far and wide.

Lis - ten to the

Chorus

mock - ing - bird, lis - ten to the mock - ing - bird, the

mock - ing - bird still sing - ing o'er her grave. Lis - ten to the

mock - ing - bird, lis - ten to the mock - ing - bird, still

1.

sing - ing where the weep - ing wil - lows wave.

2.

2. Ah, wave.

Little Brown Jug

Words and Music by Joseph E. Winner

The Lonesome Road

African-American Spiritual

Additional Lyrics

2. Look down, look down that lonesome road,
   Hang down your head and cry.
   I loved, I lost, my days are numbered.
   O Lord, I want to die.

3. Look down, look down that lonesome road,
   Where love has come and gone.
   Look up, look up, you'll find a new love.
   Look up and keep trav'lin' on.

Look for the Silver Lining

Words by Buddy DeSylva
Music by Jerome Kern

shine for you. A heart full _____ of joy and glad - ness _____ will al - ways ban - ish sad - ness and strife. _____ So al - ways look for _____ the sil - ver lin - ing _____ and try to find the sun - ny side of life. _____

The Love Nest

Words by Otto Harbach
Music by Louis A. Hirsch

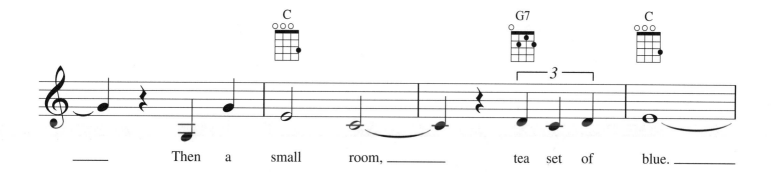

Then a small room, _____ tea set of blue. _____

Best of all room, _____ dream room for two. _____

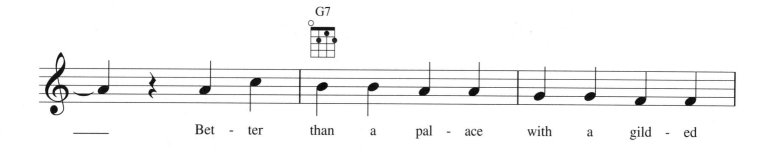

Bet - ter than a pal - ace with a gild - ed

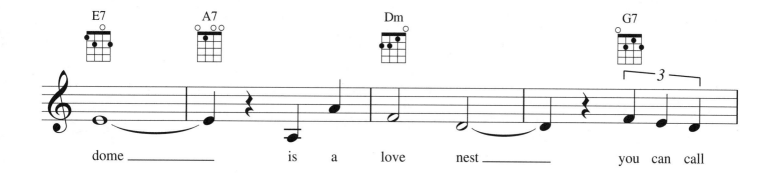

dome _____ is a love nest _____ you can call

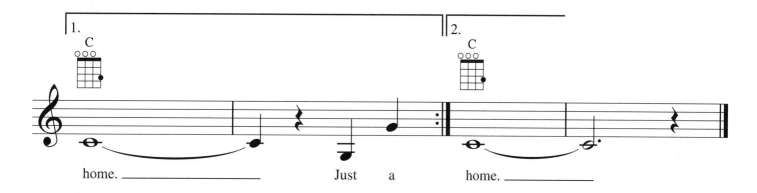

home. _____ Just a home. _____

Man of Constant Sorrow

Traditional

Mary's a Grand Old Name

Words and Music by George M. Cohan

Marine's Hymn

Words by Henry C. Davis
Melody based on a theme by Jacques Offenbach

First   to   fight   for   right   and   free -
In   the   snow   of   far - off   north - ern
If   the   ar - my   and   the   na -

dom   and   to   keep   our   hon - or   clean,
lands   and   in   sun - ny   trop - ic   scenes,
vy   ev - er   looked   on   heav - en's   scenes,

we   are   proud   to   claim   the
you   will   find   us   al - ways
they   would   find   us   the   streets   are

ti - tle   of   U - nit - ed   States   Ma -
on   the   job,   the   U - nit - ed   States   Ma -
guard - ed   by   U - nit - ed   States   Ma -

1., 2.

3.

rines.   2. Our _____ rines. _____
rines.   3. Here's __

Meet Me in St. Louis, Louis

Words by Andrew B. Sterling
Music by Kerry Mills

Melody of Love

By H. Engelmann

First note

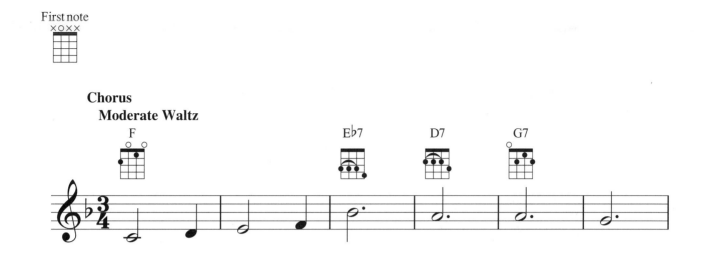

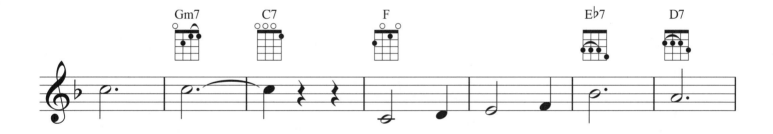

Meet Me Tonight in Dreamland

Words by Beth Slater Whitson
Music by Leo Friedman

First note

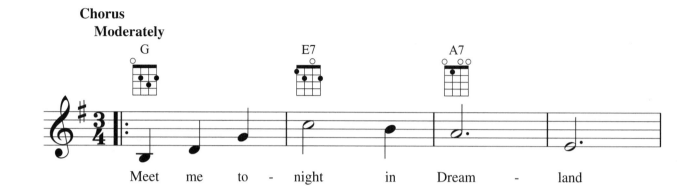

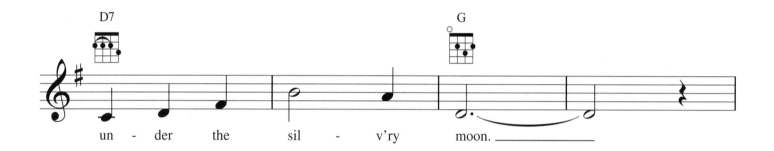

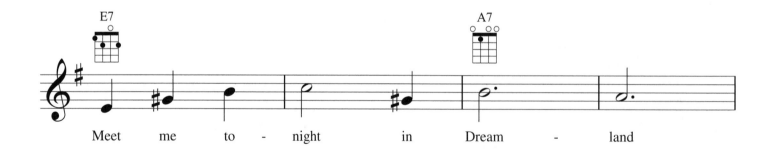

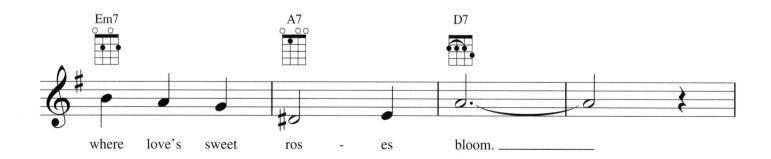

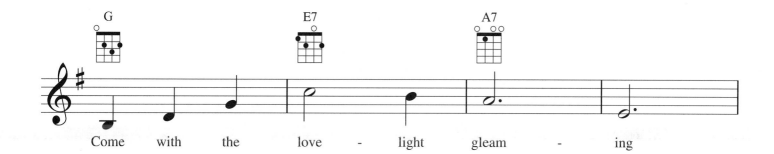

Come with the love - light gleam - ing

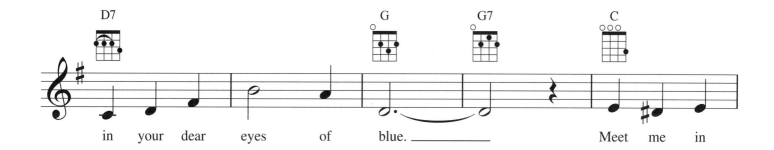

in your dear eyes of blue. _____ Meet me in

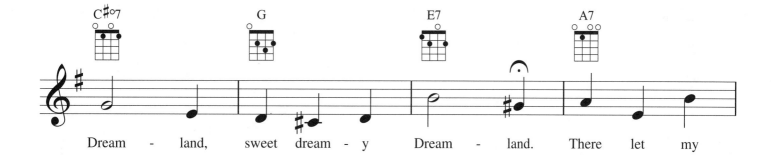

Dream - land, sweet dream - y Dream - land. There let my

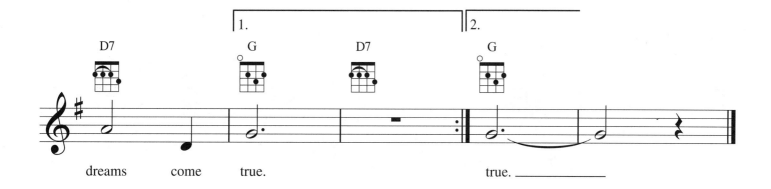

dreams come true. true. _____

97

Memories

Words by Gus Kahn
Music by Egbert Van Alstyne

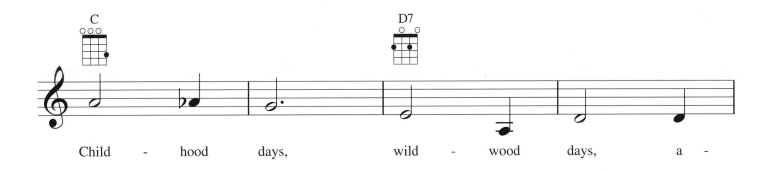

Child - hood days, wild - wood days, a -

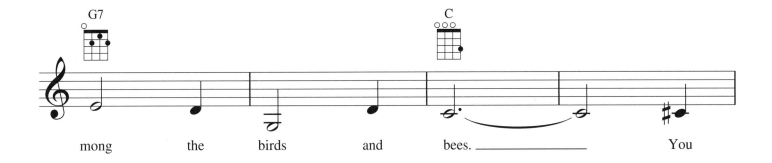

mong the birds and bees. _____ You

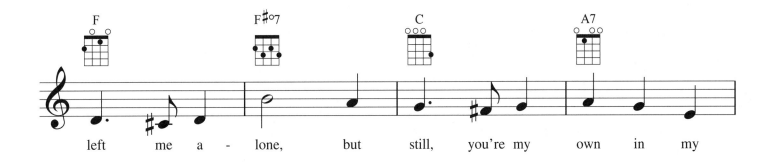

left me a - lone, but still, you're my own in my

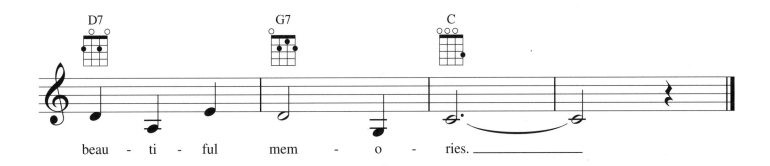

beau - ti - ful mem - o - ries. _____

Midnight Special

Railroad Song

Chorus

Spe - cial _____ shine her light ___ on me. _____

_____ Let the Mid - night Spe - cial _____ shine her ev - er - lov - in'

1.–4. light on me. ___ 2. If you ev - er go to light on me. _____

5. light on me. _____

Additional Lyrics

2. If you ever go to Houston, you'd better walk right.
   And you better not stagger and you better not fight.
   'Cause the sheriff will arrest you and he'll carry you down.
   And you can bet your bottom dollar you're Sugarland bound.

3. Yonder comes Miss Rosie; tell me, how do you know?
   I know her by her apron and the dress she wore.
   Umbrella on her shoulder, piece of paper in her hand.
   Well, I heard her tell the captain, "I want my man."

4. Lord, Thelma said she loved me, but I believe she told a lie.
   'Cause she hasn't been to see me since last July.
   She brought me little coffee, she brought me little tea,
   She brought me nearly ev'rything but the jailhouse key.

5. Well, the biscuits on the table, just as hard as any rock.
   If you try to eat them, break a convict's heart.
   My sister wrote a letter, my mother wrote a card:
   "If you want to come and see us, you'll have to ride the rods."

Moonlight Bay

Words by Edward Madden
Music by Percy Wenrich

My Buddy

Lyrics by Gus Kahn
Music by Walter Donaldson

My Melancholy Baby

Words by George Norton
Music by Ernie Burnett

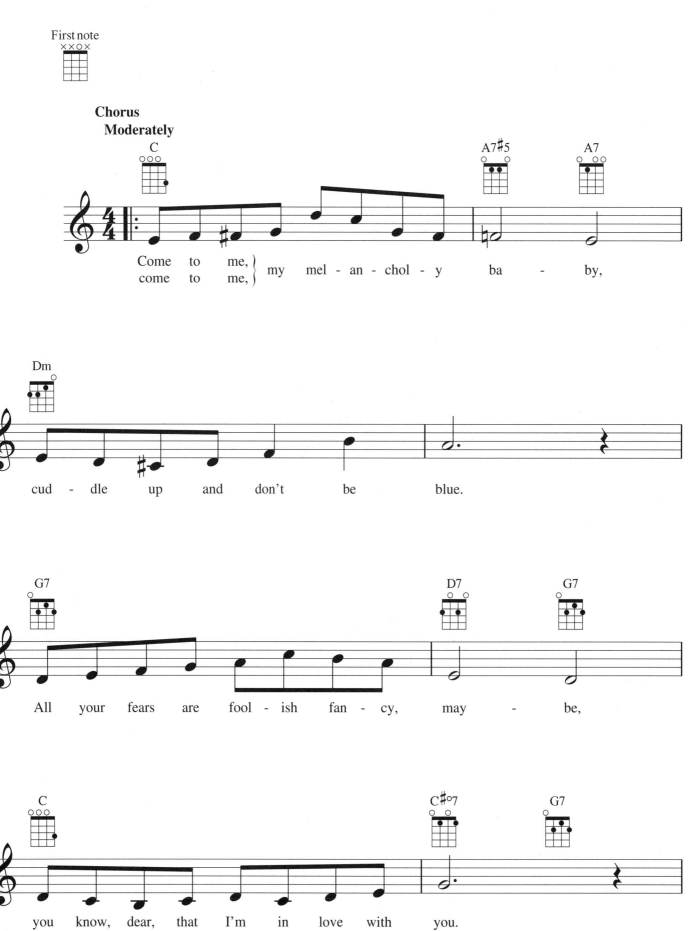

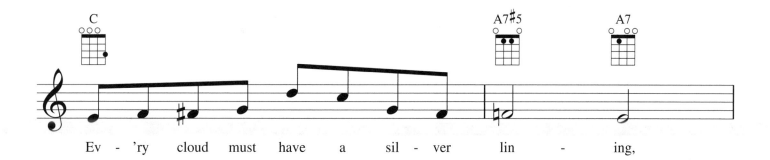

Ev - 'ry cloud must have a sil - ver lin - ing,

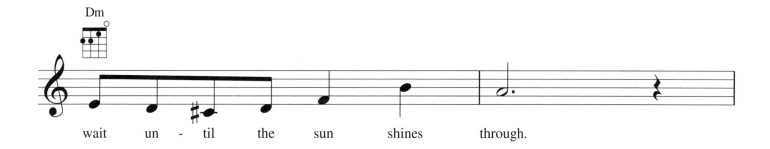

wait un - til the sun shines through.

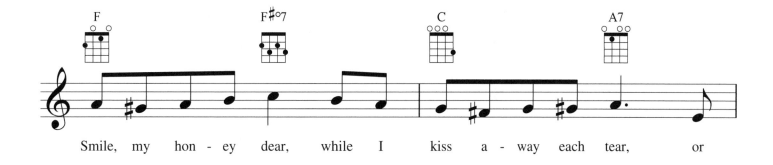

Smile, my hon - ey dear, while I kiss a - way each tear, or

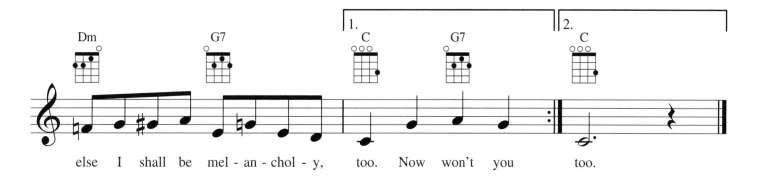

else I shall be mel - an - chol - y, too. Now won't you   too.

Oh! You Beautiful Doll

Words by A. Seymour Brown
Music by Nat D. Ayer

On Top of Old Smoky

Kentucky Mountain Folksong

First note

Verse
Moderate Waltz

1. On top of Old Smok - y, _____ all cov - ered with
2.–8. *See additional lyrics*

snow, _____ I lost my true lov - er _____

_____ by a - court - in' too slow. _____

Additional Lyrics

2. Well, a-courtin's a pleasure
   And parting is grief,
   But a false-hearted lover
   Is worse than a thief.

3. A thief, he will rob you
   And take all you have,
   But a false-hearted lover
   Will send you to your grave.

4. And the grave will decay you
   And turn you to dust.
   And where is the young man
   A poor girl can trust?

5. They'll hug you and kiss you
   And tell you more lies
   Than the cross-ties on the railroad
   Or the stars in the skies.

6. They'll tell you they love you
   Just to give your heart ease.
   But the minute your back's turned,
   They'll court whom they please.

7. So come, all you young maidens,
   And listen to me:
   Never place your affection
   On a green willow tree.

8. For the leaves, they will wither,
   And the roots, they will die,
   And your true love will leave you,
   And you'll never know why.

On a Sunday Afternoon

Words by Andrew B. Sterling
Music by Harry von Tilzer

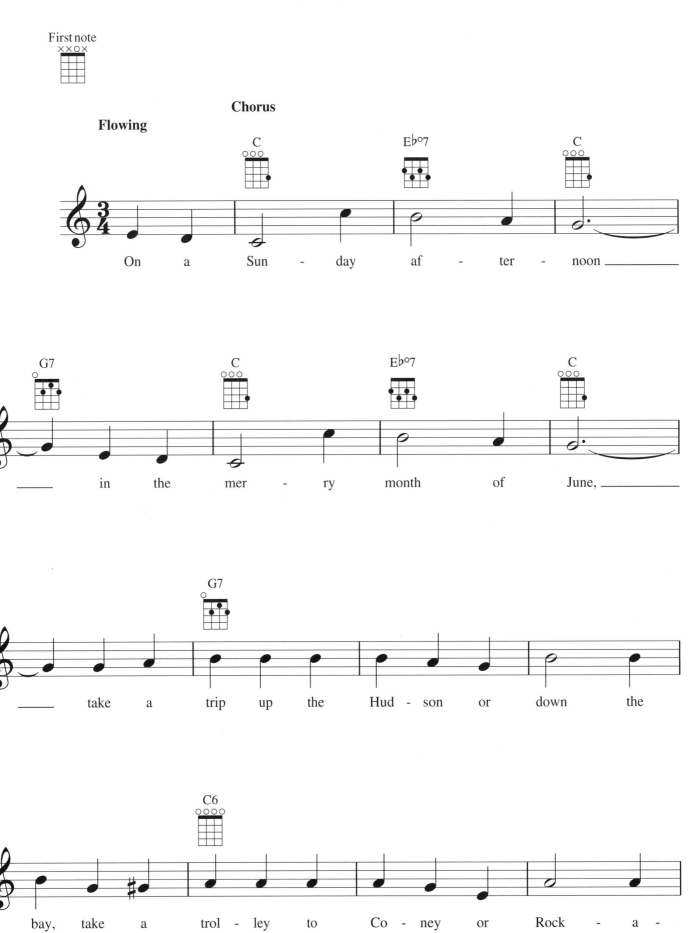

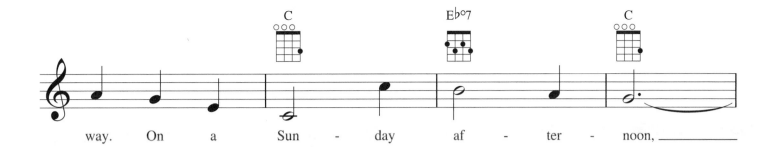

way. On a Sun - day af - ter - noon, _____

_____ you can see the lov - ers spoon. _____ They

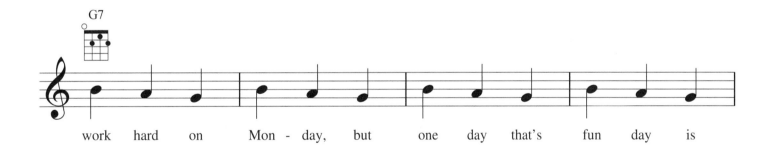

work hard on Mon - day, but one day that's fun day is

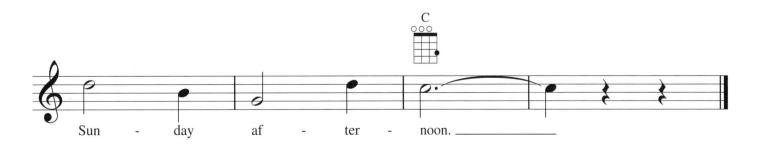

Sun - day af - ter - noon. _____

Peg o' My Heart

Words by Alfred Bryan
Music by Fred Fisher

Put Your Arms Around Me, Honey

Words by Junie McCree
Music by Albert von Tilzer

Poor Butterfly

Words by John L. Golden
Music by Raymond Hubbell

smiles through her tears, _____ she mur-murs low, _____ "The moon and I _____

_____ know that he be faith - ful; _____ I'm sure he come _____

_____ to me by and by. _____ But if he don't come back, _____

_____ then I nev - er sigh or _____ cry. _____ I just must

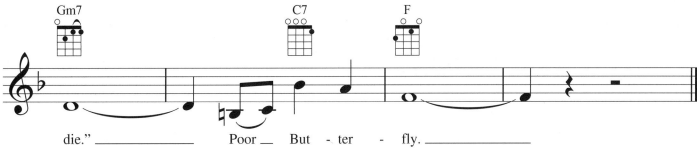

die." _____ Poor _ But - ter - fly. _____

Pretty Baby

Words by Gus Kahn
Music by Egbert Van Alstyne and Tony Jackson

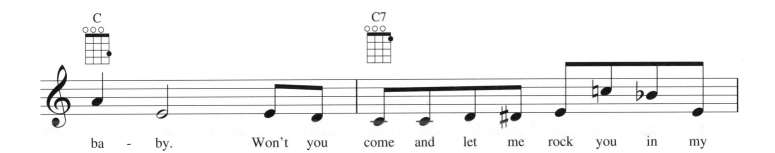

ba - by. Won't you come and let me rock you in my

cra - dle of love, ____ and we'll cud - dle all the

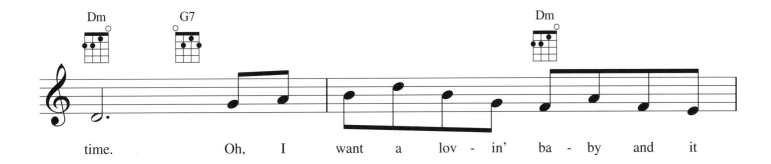

time. Oh, I want a lov - in' ba - by and it

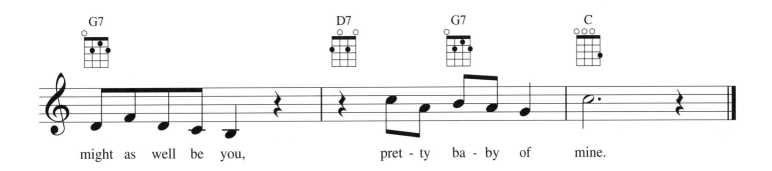

might as well be you, pret - ty ba - by of mine.

A Pretty Girl Is Like a Melody

Words and Music by Irving Berlin

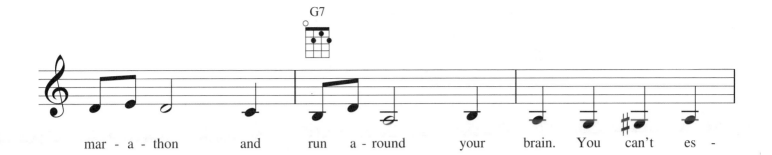

mar - a - thon   and   run a - round   your   brain.   You   can't   es -

cape; _____ she's   in   your   mem - o - ry _____ by

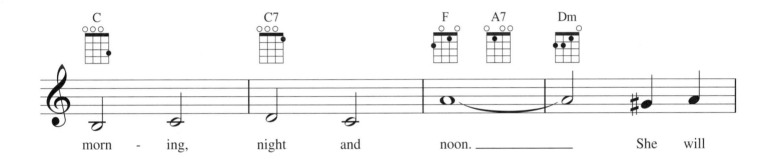

morn - ing,   night   and   noon. _____ She   will

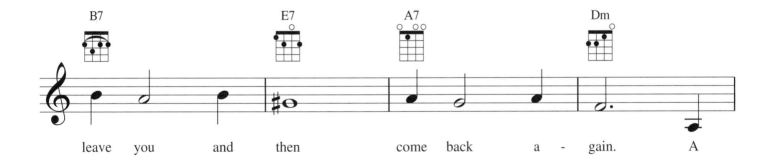

leave   you   and   then   come   back   a - gain.   A

pret - ty   girl   is   just   like   a   pret - ty   tune. _____

Rock-A-Bye Your Baby
with a Dixie Melody

Words by Sam M. Lewis and Joe Young
Music by Jean Schwartz

to Ten-nes-see with all the love that's in ___ ya. "Weep No More, My

La - dy;" sing _ that song a - gain for me, and "Old Black Joe," _

just as though _ you had _____ me on your knee. A mil-lion ba - by kiss-es

I'll de - liv - er the min-ute that you sing the "Swan-ee Riv - er."

Rock - a - bye your rock - a - bye ba - by with a Dix - ie mel - o - dy.

Rockin' Robin

Words and Music by J. Thomas

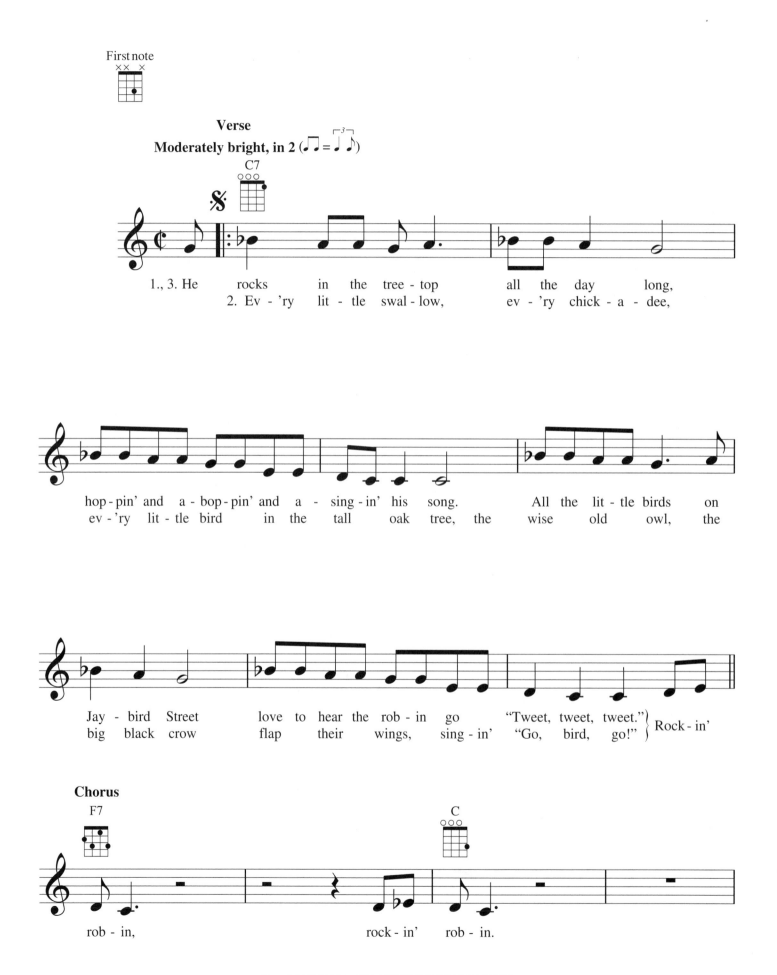

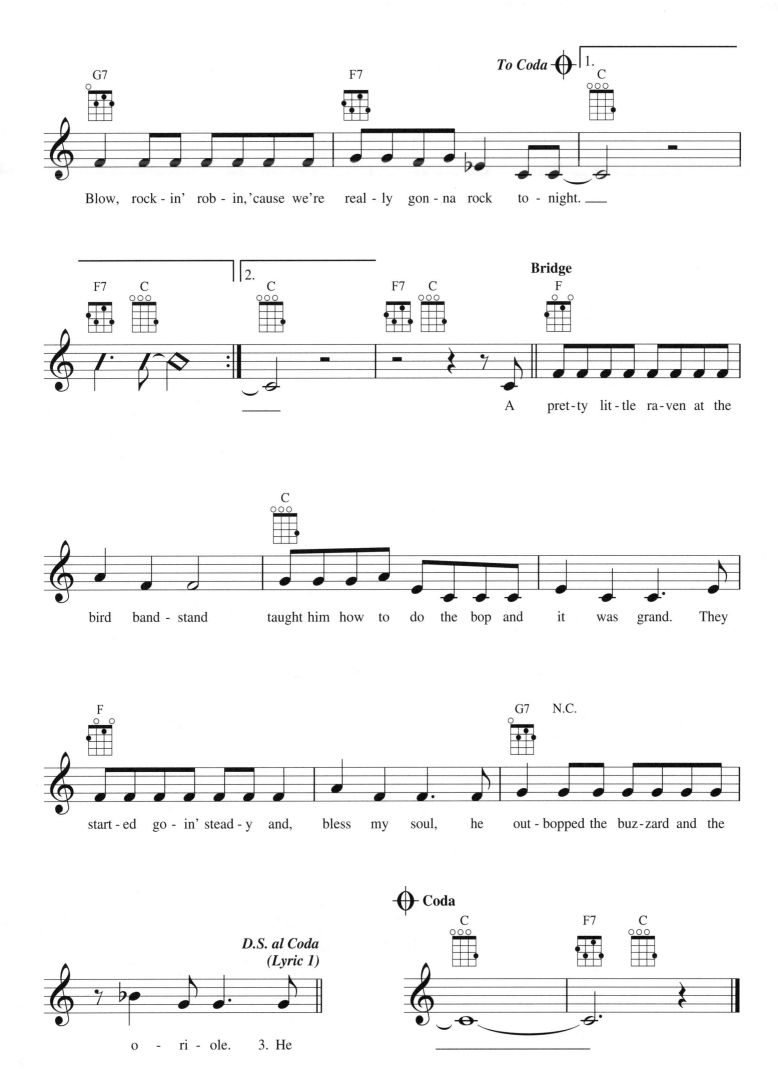

Rose Room

Words by Harry Williams
Music by Art Hickman

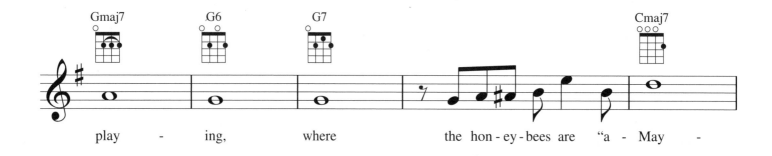

danc - ing _____ while the mead-ow brook flows. The moon when

shin - ing is more than ev - er de - sign - ing,

for 'tis ev - er then I am pin - ing,

pin - ing _____ to be sweet-ly re - clin - ing some-where in

Rose - land, be-side a beau-ti - ful rose. _____

Scarborough Fair

Traditional English

First note

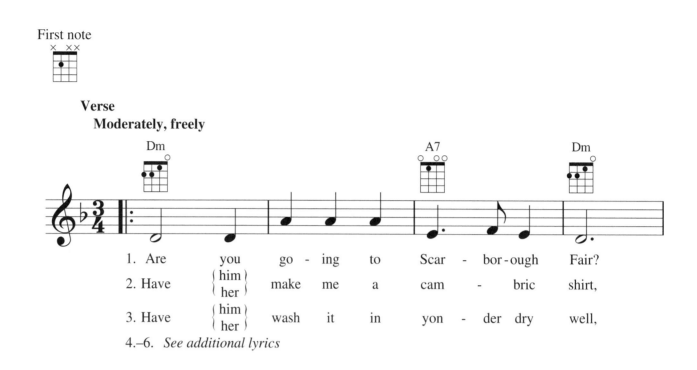

Verse
Moderately, freely

1. Are you go - ing to Scar - bor - ough Fair?
2. Have {him / her} make me a cam - bric shirt,
3. Have {him / her} wash it in yon - der dry well,
4.–6. *See additional lyrics*

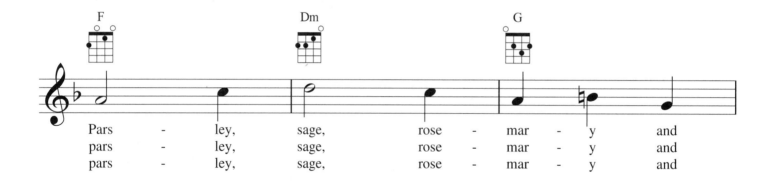

Pars - ley, sage, rose - mar - y and
pars - ley, sage, rose - mar - y and
pars - ley, sage, rose - mar - y and

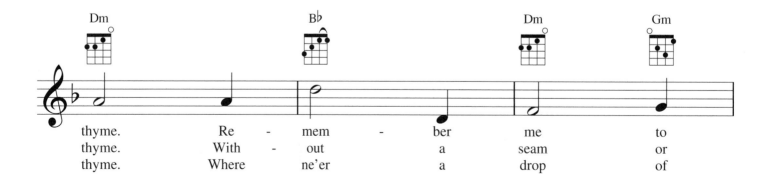

thyme. Re - mem - ber me to
thyme. With - out a seam or
thyme. Where ne'er a drop of

one	who	lives	there, _____		for	once	{ he } { she }
fine	nee -	dle -	work, _____		and	then	{ he'll } { she'll }
wa -	ter	e'er	fell, _____		and	then	{ he'll } { she'll }

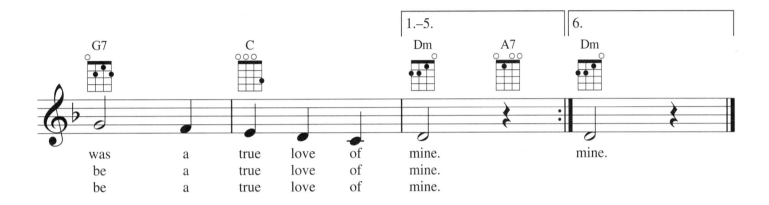

	1.–5.	6.
was a true love of mine.	mine.	
be a true love of mine.		
be a true love of mine.		

Additional Lyrics

4. Have him (her) find me an acre of land,
   Parsley, sage, rosemary and thyme.
   Between the sea and over the sand,
   And then he'll (she'll) be a true love of mine.

5. Plow the land with the horn of a lamb,
   Parsley, sage, rosemary and thyme.
   Then sow some seeds from north of the dam,
   And then he'll (she'll) be a true love of mine.

6. If he (she) tells me he (she) can't, I'll reply:
   Parsley, sage, rosemary and thyme.
   Let me know that at least he (she) will try,
   And then he'll (she'll) be a true love of mine.

Shenandoah

American Folksong

Shine On, Harvest Moon

Words by Jack Norworth
Music by Nora Bayes and Jack Norworth

Smiles

Words by J. Will Callahan
Music by Lee S. Roberts

First note

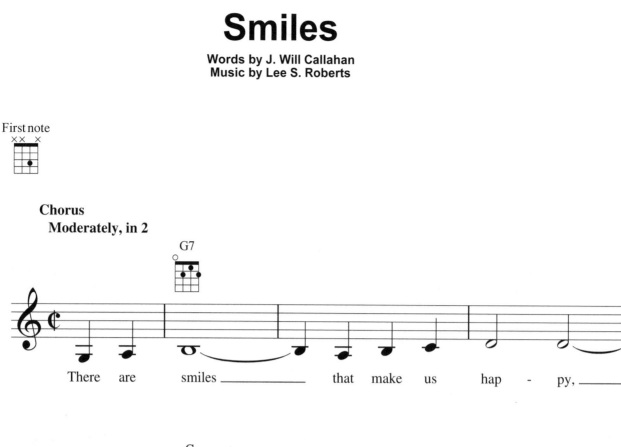

Chorus
Moderately, in 2

There are   smiles _____   that make   us   hap - py, _____

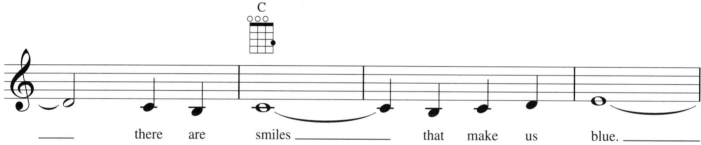

_____   there are   smiles _____   that make   us   blue. _____

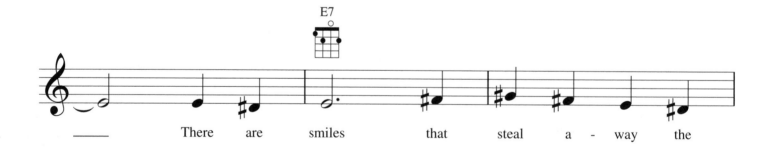

_____   There   are   smiles   that   steal   a - way   the

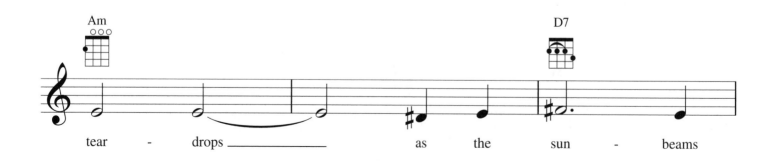

tear - drops _____   as   the   sun - beams

steal a - way the dew. _____ There are smiles that

have a ten - der mean - ing _____ that the

eyes of love a - lone may see, _____ and the

smiles that fill my life with sun - shine _____ are the

smiles that you give to me. _____

Somebody Stole My Gal

Words and Music by Leo Wood

First note

Chorus
Brightly

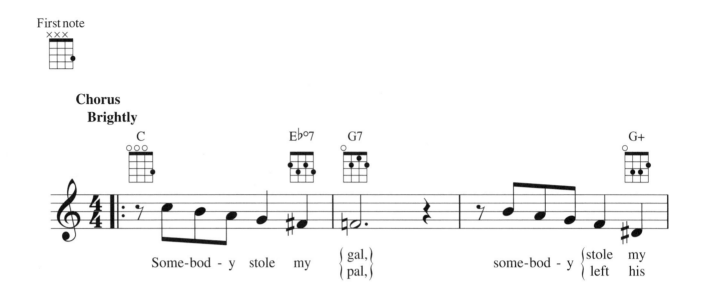

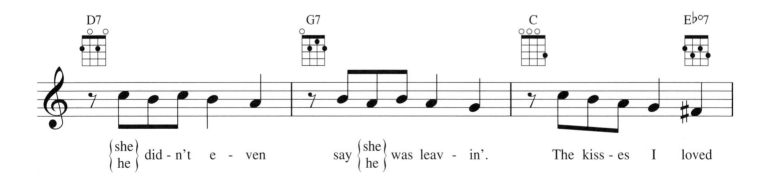

so, {he's / she's} get - ting now, I know. And

gee! _____ I know that {she _____ / he _____} would come to me _____ if {she / he} could

see {her / his} bro - ken - heart - ed lone - some {pal. / gal.}

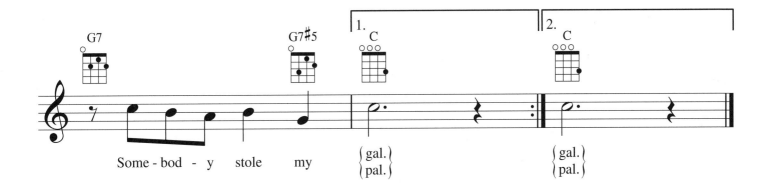

Some - bod - y stole my {gal. / pal.} {gal. / pal.}

131

Take Me Out to the Ball Game

Words by Jack Norworth
Music by Albert von Tilzer

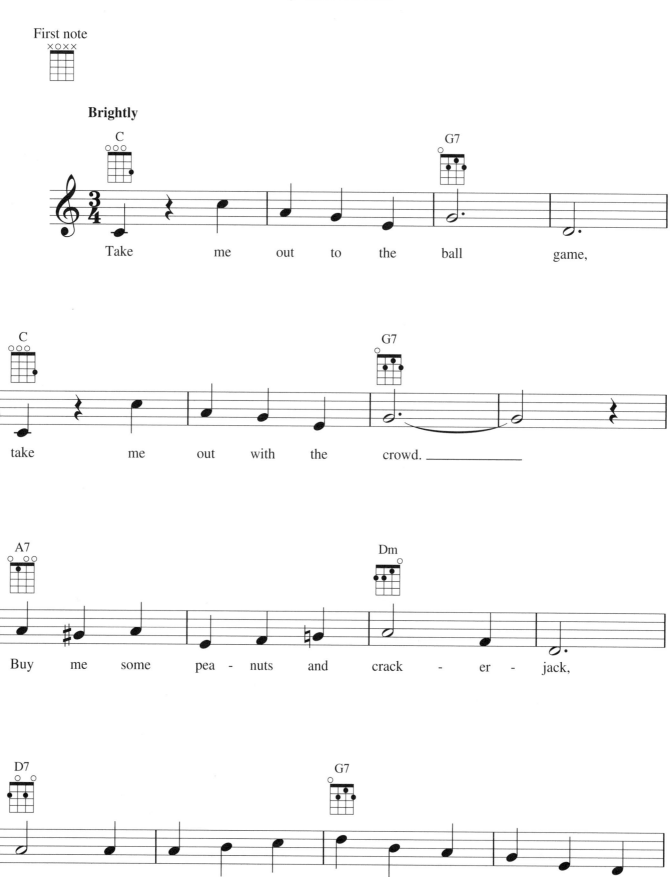

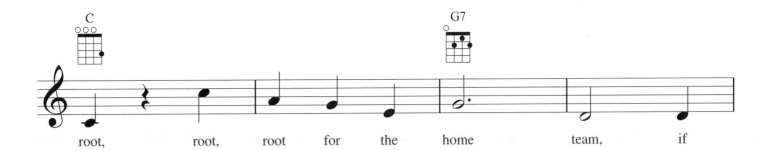

root, root, root for the home team, if

they don't win it's a shame. _____ For it's

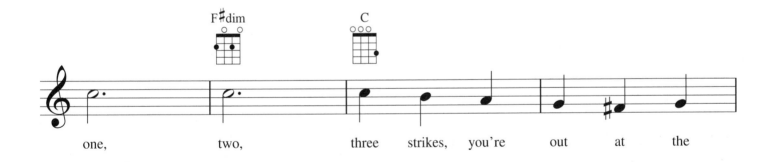

one, two, three strikes, you're out at the

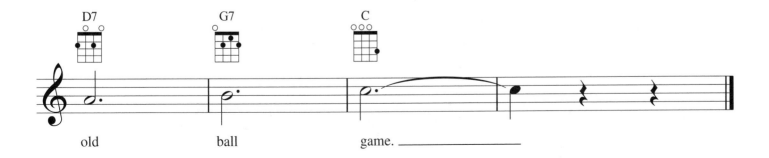

old ball game. _____

That's a Plenty

Words by Ray Gilbert
Music by Lew Pollack

do me sump - in'.   Beat it out, broth - er, there's no oth - er

rem - e - dy, _____ and that's a plen - ty, ___

plen - ty,   plen - ty for me. ___

3. Once you start, you're
4. in the mood, there

gon - na stay __ in it.   Ev - 'ry night you're out ca - fé - in' it.
ain't no stop - pin' it.   Live it, breathe it, blow your top __ in it.

1.

Swing your queen, _   what I mean, _   broth - er, you're as gone as an - y
That is jazz, _   what it has, _

2.

hu - man can be. __ And when you're   that's a plen - ty for me.

Verse

Ta-Ra-Ra-Boom-Der-E

Words and Music by Henry J. Sayers

There Is a Tavern in the Town

Traditional Drinking Song

Chorus

well, for I must leave thee. Do not let the part - ing grieve thee, and re-

mem - ber that the best of friends must part, must part. A -

dieu, a - dieu, kind friends, a - dieu, a - dieu, a - dieu. I

can no long - er stay with you, stay with you. I'll

hang my heart on a weep - ing wil - low tree, and

may the world go well with thee.

Three O'Clock in the Morning

Words by Dorothy Terriss
Music by Julian Robledo

Too-Ra-Loo-Ra-Loo-Ral

(That's an Irish Lullaby)

Words and Music by James R. Shannon

I - rish way, and I'd give the
days of yore, when she used to

world if she could sing that song to
rock me fast a - sleep out - side to the

Chorus

me this day. _____ }
cab - in door. _____ }
Too - ra - loo - ra -

loo - ral, _____ too - ra - loo - ra -

li, _____ too - ra - loo - ra - loo - ral, _____

_____ hush, now don't you cry! _____

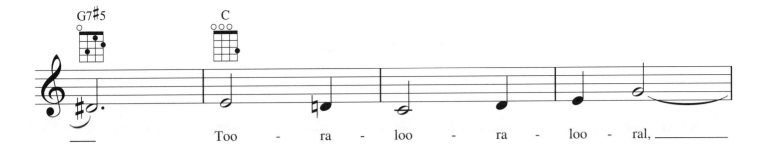

Too - ra - loo - ra - loo - ral, _____

___ too - ra - loo - ra - li, _____

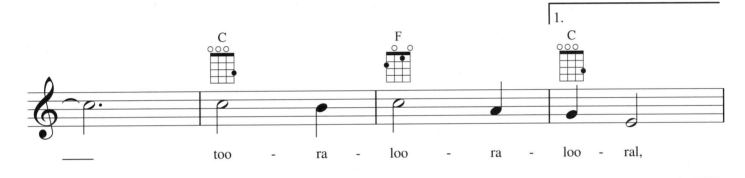

1.

___ too - ra - loo - ra - loo - ral,

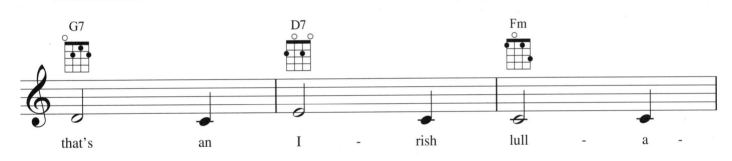

that's an I - rish lull - a -

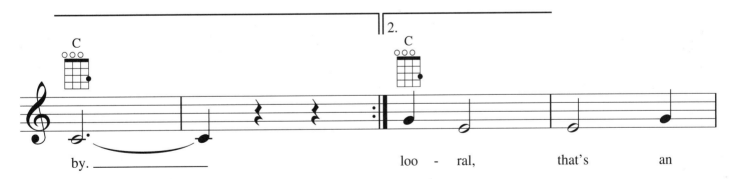

2.

by. _____ loo - ral, that's an

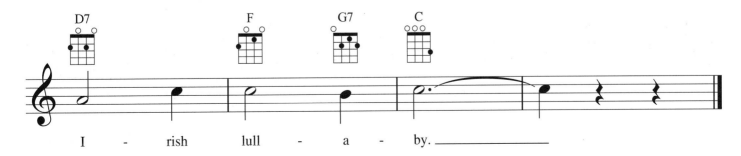

I - rish lull - a - by. _____

Tiger Rag
(Hold That Tiger)

Words by Harry DeCosta
Music by Original Dixieland Jazz Band

kick him and soak him! Where's that ti - ger?

Where's that ti - ger? Where, _____ oh, where _ can he

be? _____ Low or high - brow, they all

cry now: "Please play that Ti - ger Rag ___ for

1. me." _____   2. me." _____

Wait 'Til the Sun Shines, Nellie

Words by Andrew B. Sterling
Music by Harry von Tilzer

When Irish Eyes Are Smiling

Words by Chauncey Olcott and George Graff, Jr.
Music by Ernest R. Ball

laugh - ter's like some fair - y song, and your eyes twin - kle
life is the sweet - est of all, there is ne'er a real

C7   F   D7

bright as can be, _____ you should laugh all the
care or re - gret. _____ And while spring - time is

G   D7

while and all oth - er times, while, and now smile _____ a
ours through - out all of youth's hours, let us smile _____ each

Chorus
G   G7   C

smile for me. _____
chance we get. _____

When I - rish

G7   C   C7   F

eyes are smil - ing, _____ sure it's like a

C   F

morn in spring. _____ In the lilt of

Wayfaring Stranger

Southern American Folk Hymn

First note

With longing

Verse

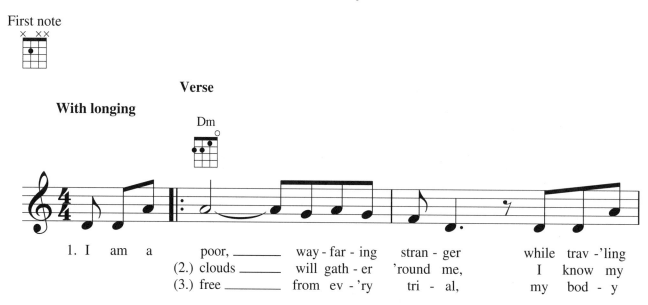

1. I am a poor, _____ way-far-ing stran-ger while trav-'ling
(2.) clouds _____ will gath-er 'round me, I know my
(3.) free _____ from ev-'ry tri-al, my bod-y

through _____ this world of woe. Yet there's no
way _____ is rough and steep. But gold-en
sleep _____ in the church-yard. I'll drop the

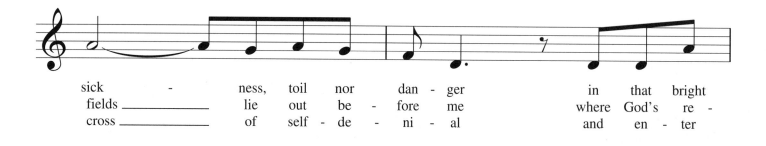

sick - ness, toil nor dan-ger in that bright
fields _____ lie out be-fore me where God's re-
cross _____ of self-de-ni-al and en-ter

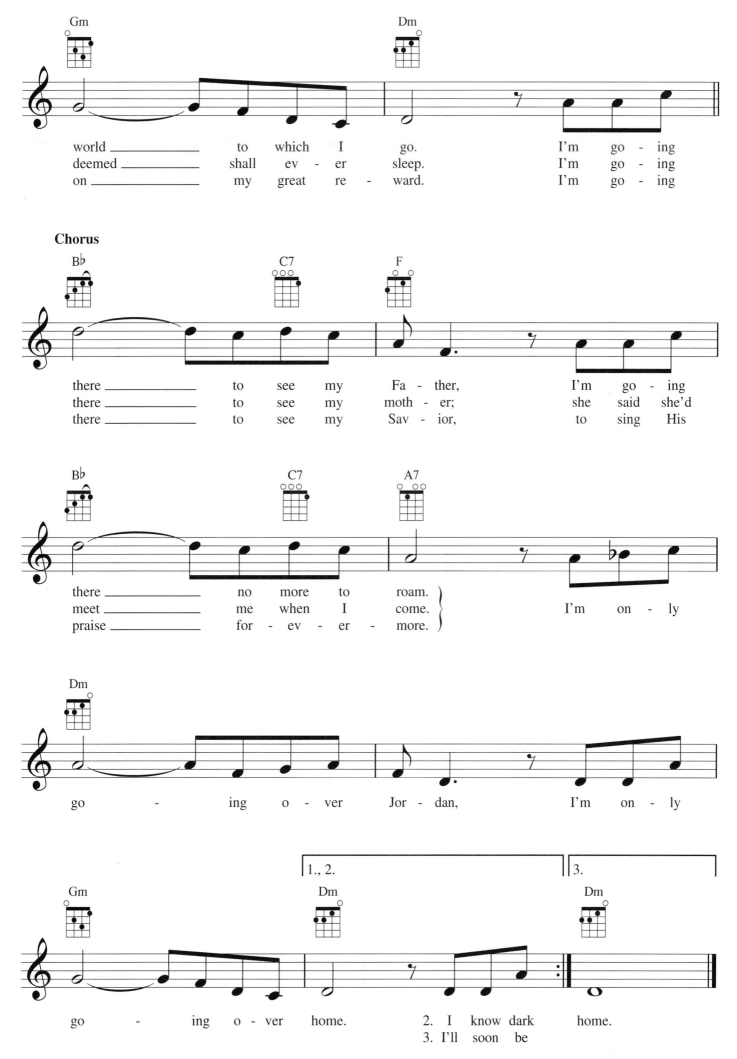

When Johnny Comes Marching Home

Words and Music by Patrick Sarsfield Gilmore

First note

Verse
Moderately

1. When John-ny comes march-ing home a-gain, hur-rah! _____ Hur-
2.–4. *See additional lyrics*

rah! _____ We'll give him a heart-y wel-come then, hur-rah! _____ Hur-

rah! _____ Oh, the men will cheer and the boys will shout. The la-dies, they _ will

all turn out. And we'll all feel gay when John-ny comes march-ing home. _____

Additional Lyrics

2. Get ready for the Jubilee, hurrah! Hurrah!
   We'll give the hero three times three, hurrah! Hurrah!
   The laurel wreath is ready now
   To place upon his loyal brow.
   And we'll all feel gay when
   Johnny comes marching home.

3. The old church bell will peal with joy, hurrah! Hurrah!
   To welcome home our darling boy, hurrah! Hurrah!
   The village lads and lassies say,
   With roses they will strew the way,
   And we'll all feel gay when
   Johnny comes marching home.

4. Let love and friendship on that day, hurrah! Hurrah!
   Their choicest treasures then display, hurrah! Hurrah!
   And let each one perform some part
   To fill with joy the warrior's heart.
   And we'll all feel gay when
   Johnny comes marching home.

When the Saints Go Marching In

Words by Katherine E. Purvis
Music by James M. Black

Additional Lyrics

2. Oh, when the sun refuse to shine,
   Oh, when the sun refuse to shine,
   Oh, Lord, I want to be in that number,
   When the sun refuse to shine.

3. Oh, when the stars have disappeared,
   Oh, when the stars have disappeared,
   Oh, Lord, I want to be in that number,
   When the stars have disappeared.

3. Oh, when the day of judgment comes,
   Oh, when the day of judgment comes,
   Oh, Lord, I want to be in that number,
   When the day of judgment comes.

While Strolling Through the Park One Day

Words and Music by Ed Haley and Robert A. Keiser

Of course, we were as hap-py as can be.

Outro-Chorus

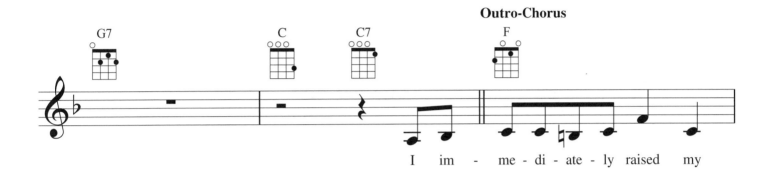

I im - me - di - ate - ly raised my

hat, and fi - nal - ly ___ she re - marked. I ___

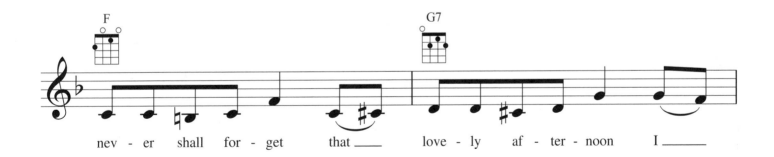

nev - er shall for - get that ___ love - ly af - ter - noon I ___

met her at the foun - tain in the park.

Whispering

Words and Music by Richard Coburn, John Schonberger and Vincent Rose

The World Is Waiting for the Sunrise

Words by Eugene Lockhart
Music by Ernest Seitz

You Tell Me Your Dream

Words by Seymour Rice and Albert H. Brown
Music by Charles N. Daniels

Yankee Doodle Boy

Words and Music by George M. Cohan

First note

Chorus
March tempo, in 2

I'm a Yan - kee Doo - dle dan - dy, a Yan - kee Doo - dle, do or die; _____ a real live neph - ew of my Un - cle Sam's,

born on the Fourth of Ju - ly. _____ I've

got a Yan - kee Doo - dle sweet - heart,

she's my Yan - kee Doo - dle joy. _____

Yan - kee Doo - dle came to Lon - don just to ride the po - nies.

I am the Yan - kee Doo - dle boy. _____

The Yellow Rose of Texas

Words and Music by J.K., 1858

You're a Grand Old Flag

Words and Music by George M. Cohan

First note

Chorus
March tempo, in 2

You're a grand old flag, you're a

high-fly-ing flag, and for-ev-er in

peace may you wave. You're the

em-blem of the land I

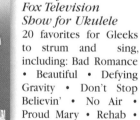